D1592449

THE ETERNAL TRUTHS *of*
NARNIA

Bridge-Logos

Alachua, Florida 32615

THE ETERNAL TRUTHS *of*

NARNIA

BIBLE STUDIES AND LEADER'S GUIDE

From *The Chronicles of Narnia*

By JULIE KLOSTER

Bridge-Logos

Alachua, Florida 32615

Bridge-Logos

Alachua, Florida 32615

The Eternal Truths of Narnia: Bible Studies and Leader's Guide from The Chronicles of Narnia

by Julie Kloster

This study first appeared on ChristianBibleStudies.com.

Copyright © 2008 by Bridge-Logos

All rights reserved. Under International Copyright Law, no portion of this book may be reproduced, stored in a retrieval system, or transmitted in any form or by any means—electronic, mechanical, photographic (photocopy), recording, scanning, or other—except for brief quotations in critical reviews or articles, without the prior written permission from the Publisher.

Printed in Canada.

Library of Congress Catalog Card Number: 2008925259
International Standard Book Number: 978-0-88270-616-0

Unless otherwise noted all Scripture quotations are taken from the *Holy Bible, New International Version*® NIV®. Copyright © 1973, 1978, 1984 by International Bible Society. Used by permission of Zondervan. All rights reserved.

G532.316.N.m803.352100

❧ CONTENTS ❧

IN THE BEGINNING

BOOK: THE MAGICIAN'S NEPHEW

The sovereignty of the Creator is revealed in the magical beginnings of Narnia.

C.S. Lewis weaves a magical, humorous, and touching journey of adventures to unknown worlds into his story about a boy who is grieving for his ill mother. Throughout the battle between good and evil, Lewis ultimately reveals the sovereign workings of the Creator. This concept can be related to our struggles with grief and the consequences of sin on the earth.

Unearthing the Deeper Meaning and Truth

How does God, in His sovereignty, use all things for the good of His people and the glory of His name? What are the effects of sin on creation? How do we deal with temptation? Why does God allow pain and suffering? This study guide will help you unearth the deeper meanings and eternal truths that C.S. Lewis wove into his magical story of Creation.

Scriptures:

Genesis 1; 3:1–7, 24; Isaiah 40:6–31; Psalm 139:1–18; John 11:1–44; Romans 1:18–22; 11:33–36; 1 Corinthians 1:18–31; 10:13; Colossians 2:8–9.

Based on:

The Magician's Nephew, C.S. Lewis (Macmillan Publishing Company, 1955)

PART 1

BOOK SUMMARY: *THE MAGICIAN'S NEPHEW*

✐ *Note to leader: Prior to the class, provide for each person the book,* THE MAGICIAN'S NEPHEW *by C.S. Lewis.*

Digory is a young boy living with his aunt and evil uncle; his mother is dying and needs the care of these family members. Over the neighborhood wall in London he meets Polly. In their explorations the children accidentally stumble into the forbidden attic of Digory's uncle. Uncle Andrew uses magical, glowing rings to tempt Polly, so he can send her into a spatial dimension that he is afraid to explore himself. When Polly disappears as she touches the ring, Digory immediately shows his character by purposefully following her into this unknown and frightening dimension. He chooses to protect and help her, even though he does not know if he will ever return.

Digory and Polly see the drastic and horrible consequences of sin in the frozen, old world of Charn. Digory gives into the temptation to ring a bell that has a warning inscription and brings the white witch, Queen Jadis, back to life from her frozen state. The witch follows them back to their own world, creating havoc wherever she goes. In their attempts to return the white witch to Charn, they inadvertently bring her to Narnia instead. This introduces evil to Narnia, a new land just being created by Aslan.

Digory realizes Aslan has the power to heal his mother. He finds the courage to approach Aslan, and in this encounter Digory and Polly begin to understand the great love of God and His sovereign working throughout all of life. Instead of immediately healing Digory's mother, however, Aslan sends him on a journey to find a seed, which will grow into a tree that will protect Narnia from the white witch. Digory faces temptation in the garden that contains the seed, much like Adam and Eve faced temptation in the Garden of Eden. Digory finds the strength and grace to withstand the temptation and returns the fruit to Aslan. The tree is planted, and when the tree produces fruit, Aslan gives it to Digory to take back to his mother for healing.

PART 2

DISCOVER THE ETERNAL PRINCIPLES

☛ **Teaching Point One:** God spoke the world into existence, and He continues to speak to us today.

■ Read Genesis 1 and Romans 1:18–22.

In *The Magician's Nephew,* Aslan called life into existence through his song. Similarly, Genesis 1 says God spoke Creation into existence. The intricacies, power, and beauty of Creation speak to us about our Creator. The book of Romans says that because of nature, we have no excuse to not know God.

God's Word has been the call to life since paradise. He continues to speak to us today. His written Word, the Bible, is alive and powerful to call us to himself and to change our lives. Today, His call to man is a summons to new life in Christ. When we read His Word, He speaks to us directly and intimately. His Word brings comfort and peace, as well as conviction and reproof.

Question 1: Genesis 1 says God spoke Creation into existence. How did God feel about what He had created? How does God speak to His Creation (including to us) today? How is what God created different from anything man creates?

_____

_____

_____

_____

_____

Leader's Note: God is the only One who creates out of nothing. Man creates out of things already in existence.

Question 2: What does Romans mean when it says because of nature we are without excuse? What does nature tell you about God?

_____

_____

_____

_____

Leader's Note: Consider the beauty, intricacy, and interdependence of life, as well as its power in the form of storms and natural disasters.

Aslan called Creation into existence with his song. His song had different effects on each person. Cabby, Digory, and Polly had open mouths and shining eyes as they drank in the sound of Aslan's song. Polly felt sure what she heard was a call, and that "anyone who heard that call would want to obey it." The horse tried harder to listen and looked younger and more alert. Uncle Andrew shook when he heard Aslan's voice and did not like it. He wanted to get away from it. "The longer and more beautifully the lion sang, the harder Uncle Andrew tried to believe he could hear nothing but roaring." The witch understood it, but it made her angry, and she hated it.

Question 3: How do people respond in different ways to God's Word today? Why do people respond differently? Why is God's Word so powerful? How is the power of God's voice reflected in each of the above character's reactions?

_____

_____

_____

_____

Question 4: Read Psalm 139:1–18. What does Psalm 139 tell us about how God created us? According to this passage, what does God know about us? What does this passage imply about God's great love and care for you? What does it imply about God's care for the details in your life?

_____

_____

_____

_____

Question 5: How does the author of this Psalm respond to God? The Bible says God knows how many hairs are on our head (Matthew 10:30), searches our hearts, and understands every intent of our thoughts (Job 21:27). Before there is a word on our tongue, He knows it all (Psalm 139:4). How do you feel, knowing your Creator knows you better than you know yourself?

_____

_____

Question 6: 2 Corinthians 5:17 says if we are in Christ, we are a new creation. C.S. Lewis described this transformation in these words, "Their faces had a new expression, especially the King's. All the sharpness and cunning and quarrelsomeness which he had picked up as a London cabby seemed to have been washed away, and the courage and kindness which he had always had were easier to see. Perhaps it was the air of the young world that had done it, or talking with Aslan, or both." What does it mean that we are new creatures? How do God's Word and His presence transform us into new creatures, so that we are more like Christ? What attributes should new creatures in Christ exhibit?

_____

_____

_____

_____

_____

☛ Teaching Point Two: Relativism and rationalization lead to sin and misery.

■ Read James 1:13–16, 1 Corinthians 1:18–31 and reread Romans 1:18–23.

Relativism is the theory that all truth is relative to the individual and to the time or place in which he acts, according to *The American Heritage Dictionary of the English Language.* Relativism is deciding which of God's laws apply to us. It is born of a desire to do things our own way. Rationalization is defined as devising self-satisfying, but incorrect reasons for one's behavior (*The American Heritage Dictionary of the English Language*). It is justifying why we think we do not need to obey God's laws. Each of these methods is exchanging God's truth for a lie (Romans 1:25) and leads to sin. Sin begins in our thoughts. When we let evil thoughts take hold, instead of taking every thought captive (2 Corinthians 10:5), it gives birth to sin. Sin leads to devastating consequences to self and others, and eventually brings death.

■ Read the beginning of Chapter 2 where Uncle Andrew defends his actions to Digory.

Question 7: How did Uncle Andrew use relativism to rationalize why he broke his promise to Mrs. Lefay? What was Digory's first impression of Uncle Andrew's story? Why was Digory almost taken in by Uncle Andrew's speech? What helped Digory to see the truth?

_____

_____

_____

_____

_____

Question 8: Do you agree with Digory's definition of Uncle Andrew's relativism when he said, "All it means is that he thinks he can do anything he likes to get anything he wants"? Explain your answer. Do you think Uncle Andrew truly believed the rules did not apply to him? When we suppress truth, do we truly believe the lies we tell ourselves and others? Support your viewpoint.

_____

_____

_____

_____

_____

_____

_____

Question 9: How did relativism and rationalization affect Uncle Andrew's choices? What was Uncle Andrew's true character?

_____

_____

_____

_____

_____

Question 10: Read the section of Chapter 5 where Queen Jadis justifies her actions to Digory and Polly. How does Queen Jadis use relativism and rationalization to explain her choices and behavior? Do you agree with Jadis that what is wrong for some people may not be wrong for others? Explain your answer. What would be the result if certain people were freed from all rules, as Jadis claimed she was free?

_____

_____

_____

_____

_____

_____

_____

_____

_____

Question 11: According to the book of Romans, how does man suppress truth in unrighteousness? What are the results of suppressing the truth (Romans 1:18)? How do rationalization and relativism suppress the truth?

_____

_____

_____

_____

_____

_____

_____

Question 12: Why does Romans say we are without excuse? According to Romans 1:21, what leads us to futile speculations? What are the results of these futile speculations?

_____

_____

_____

_____

_____

Question 13: How did Uncle Andrew and Queen Jadis profess to be wise, but truly become foolish, as Romans 1:22 describes? How did Uncle Andrew and Queen Jadis exchange God's truth for a lie? Who did they worship instead of God?

_____

_____

_____

_____

_____

Question 14: Aslan told the children that Uncle Andrew thought great folly, meaning his thoughts were wrong and foolish in light of the truth. What were some of Uncle Andrew's foolish thoughts? What were the results of Andrew's futile thinking?

_____

_____

_____

_____

_____

Question 15: According to 1 Corinthians, what does God think of the wisdom of mankind? What is the wisdom of mankind? How does it differ from the wisdom of God? Why does God consider the wisdom of mankind foolishness?

_____

_____

_____

_____

_____

_____

Question 16: Aslan decided the cabbie and his wife should be the king and queen of Narnia. The cabbie was surprised because he had not had much education. Similarly, Jesus called fishermen to be his disciples. According to 1 Corinthians, why does God often choose whom the world considers foolish, weak, and despised to do His work?

_____

_____

_____

_____

_____

Question 17: Aslan said he could not comfort Uncle Andrew because he made himself unable to hear Aslan's voice. Is it possible to harden our hearts so that we do not hear God's voice? Why do we harden our hearts to God's voice? What do you think Aslan meant when he said, "Oh Adam's sons, how cleverly you defend yourselves against all that might do you good!"?

_____

_____

_____

_____

_____

_____

_____

_____

_____

_____

Question 18: Aslan gave Uncle Andrew sleep to give him rest from all the torments he had desired for himself. How do we desire torments for ourselves?

_____

_____

_____

_____

_____

_____

_____

Question 19: What does the book of James say is the cause of sin? What is the ultimate result of sin, according to James? Why does James warn us to not be deceived? Were Andrew and Jadis deceived? Support your answer.

_____

_____

_____

_____

_____

_____

_____

_____

_____

_____

☞Teaching Point Three: Satan tempts us at our weakest points, but God gives us the power to overcome.

■ Read Genesis 3:1–7, 24; 1 Corinthians 10:13; and Colossians 2:8–9.

Genesis tells us Satan is crafty. He tells us half-truths to deceive us, and he tempts us at our weakest points. He prowls about like a roaring lion seeking whom he may devour (1 Peter 5:8). God promises, however, that we will never be tempted beyond what we are able to endure. He is faithful to provide a way of escape.

■ Read the section of Chapter 13 where Digory enters the garden to retrieve the apple for Aslan.

Question 20: What prevented Digory from biting the apple when he first entered the garden? What is implied about the bird? How was the bird a way of escape for Digory?

_____

_____

_____

_____

_____

_____

_____

_____

_____

Question 21: What half-truths did the witch tell Digory? How did she play on Digory's doubts and fears? How did she use false guilt to manipulate his emotions?

_____

_____

_____

_____

_____

Question 22: Digory told the witch that he did not want to live on earth forever, but that he would rather live an ordinary length of time on earth, and then die and go to heaven. Do you agree with Digory that death is better than living forever on earth? Explain your answer.

_____

_____

_____

_____

_____

Question 23: In Genesis 3:24 it says that God left an angel to guard the tree of life so that no one could eat of it. This prevented people from living forever on earth. Why was it merciful of God to keep us from living forever on earth (_consider the fallen state of man and sin on earth_)? What would life be like if we lived forever here? How does it compare to eternity in heaven where there is no more sorrow, pain, or suffering?

_____

_____

_____

_____

_____

_____

_____

_____

_____

_____

_____

Question 24: Digory's major temptation was to disobey Aslan and take the apple to his mother, instead of back to Aslan to protect Narnia. What kept Digory from giving in to the witch's temptation? Why did remembering the tears in Aslan's eyes, when Digory spoke to Aslan about his mother, make him feel sure he had done the right thing?

_____

_____

_____

_____

_____

_____

_____

_____

_____

_____

Question 25: Aslan explained to Digory that getting your heart's desire through disobedience brings misery. Do you agree with this? Discuss your answer.

_____

_____

_____

_____

_____

_____

Question 26: In Genesis 3 what lies or half-truths did Satan tell Eve? Why are half-truths deceptive?

_____

_____

_____

_____

_____

_____

_____

Question 27: According to Colossians, how do philosophy and empty deception take us captive? How can we guard against it? How did Satan use this with Eve in the Garden of Eden? How does he attempt to use it with us today? Give practical examples.

_____

_____

_____

_____

_____

_____

_____

_____

_____

_____

☛ **Teaching Point Four: God's ways are higher than our ways.**

■ Read Isaiah 40:6–31, Romans 11:33–36, and John 11:32–44.

God's wisdom and knowledge are so deep and rich that we cannot even fathom them. We cannot search or figure out His judgments. No one knows the mind of God or why He does what He does. God answers to no one, for He is God, and we are not. When we do not understand His ways, we must trust His heart. He loves us with an everlasting love, and He promises believers to work out all things for our good and His glory. He is in control of all things, and our ways are not hidden from Him. He is never weary or tired, and His understanding is inscrutable.

■ Read the section of Chapter 12 where Digory asks Aslan to cure his mother. When Digory asked Aslan to cure his mother, he was surprised to see Aslan's eyes full of tears of grief and compassion. Digory began to understand that Aslan cared more about his mother than he did himself. Instead of offering healing, however, Aslan sent Digory on a journey to protect Narnia from the evil that Digory had been responsible for bringing into the land. Digory did not understand Aslan's ways, but he began to trust his heart.

Scripture tells us that Jesus wept when Lazarus died. Since Jesus knew Lazarus was going to be raised from the dead, His grief must have been for Mary and Martha's pain and the ravages of sin on earth that produce death and grief. We will never fully understand God's ways or why He allows suffering, pain, and grief. When we do not understand His ways, we must trust His heart.

Question 28: How do you believe God feels about our sorrow? Jesus was a man of sorrows and acquainted with grief (Isaiah 53:3). Does it help you to know God understands your pain? Explain your answer.

_____

_____

_____

_____

_____

_____

_____

Question 29: C.S. Lewis said, "It is not that we doubt that God will do the best thing for us, it is that we are wondering how painful His best will be." What do you think about this statement?

_____

_____

_____

_____

Question 30: Digory did not know how he was to accomplish the task God gave him, but after talking to Aslan, he knew he could do whatever Aslan called him to do. Why should being in God's presence give us the peace, courage, strength, and knowledge to realize we can do anything God calls us to do?

_____

_____

_____

_____

Question 31: How do you think Digory felt when Aslan did not immediately heal his mother? How did Martha and Mary feel when Jesus did not come in time to heal Lazarus? How did Jesus respond to their grief? Why did Jesus say He had delayed in coming (John 11:4–6)?

_____

_____

_____

_____

Question 32: When Digory brought the fruit back to Aslan, he confessed his temptation to take the fruit to his mother instead of bringing it to Aslan for the healing of Narnia. Aslan told Digory the results of that would have been disastrous for Narnia and his mother. "There might be things more terrible even than losing someone you love to death," Aslan told Digory. What is more terrible than death?

_____

_____

Question 33: Why is it difficult to trust God during difficult times? What promises must we claim at times like this?

_____

_____

_____

_____

_____

Question 34: When Digory returned with the fruit for Aslan, Aslan said, "Well done." Digory found he had forgotten his troubles and was absolutely content when he was in Aslan's presence. Share a time with your group when you had God's peace that passes understanding during a time of crisis, because you were spending time in God's presence.

_____

_____

_____

_____

Question 35: At the end of the book Aslan did heal Digory's mother through his own plan, much as Lazarus was raised from the dead. In both cases, however, the healing did not give them life everlasting on earth, and they eventually died. Why do you think God heals sometimes and not others?

_____

_____

_____

_____

✐ _Leader's Note: It is all dependent on His will and plan for each of our lives, and how He desires to work things for our good and His glory._

PART 3

THE CLOSING CHAPTER

C.S. Lewis wove a delightful story that demonstrates the truth of God's sovereign reign over all of Creation. His characters represent the various personalities of man. Through this humorous and compelling story of God's truth, we recognize ourselves and remember the great love and mercy of our Creator.

Questions for the Closing Chapter

Question 1: What did you find to be the most powerful passage of this book?

_____

Question 2: Which character did you relate to the most? Why did you relate to him or her?

_____

_____

_____

Question 3: What new thoughts about Creation do you now have because of reading this book?

_____

_____

_____

Question 4: What new thoughts about God's sovereignty has this book helped reveal to you?

_____

_____

_____

Question 5: What additional themes or messages did you notice in this book?

_____

_____

_____

_____

_____

_____

[] *Optional Activities*

▲ *Compare and contrast Genesis 1 with the creation of Narnia.*

▲ *Compare and contrast the temptation of Eve in Genesis 3 with the temptation of Digory in the garden.*

Additional Resources

ChristianBibleStudies.com

Beyond The Wardrobe: The Official Guide to Narnia, E. J. Kirk (Zondervan Corp., 2005; ISBN: 0060765534)

Companion to Narnia, Revised Edition, Paul F. Ford (Harpercollins Publishing; ISBN: 0060791276)

Exploring The Lion, The Witch And The Wardrobe, Devin Brown (Baker, 2005; ISBN: 0801065992)

A Field Guide To Narnia, Colin Duriez (Intervarsity Press, 2004; ISBN: 0830832076)

The Heart of Narnia, Thomas Williams (Thomas Nelson/W, 2005; ISBN: 0849904889)

Step Into Narnia: A Journey Through The Lion, The Witch and the Wardrobe (Zondervan Corp., 2005; ISBN: 0060572132)

THE TRIUMPH OVER EVIL

BOOK: THE LION, THE WITCH, AND THE WARDROBE

How does the deeper magic of Narnia, from before time began,
reveal God's magnificent plan for salvation?

An enchanted wardrobe opens a porthole to Narnia. Four children, who are part of the fulfillment of prophecy to save Narnia from the evil of the White Witch, enter through it. They find Narnia in endless winter and Aslan's magical creatures under her evil control. C. S. Lewis parallels the crucifixion of Christ in this dramatic, moving, and breathtaking story of salvation.

Unearthing the Deeper Meaning and Truth

How do lust and self-deception lead to sin? What are the ultimate results of sin? Why was Jesus willing to die in our place? How did His death bring us intimacy with God? How does the resurrection of Christ show us God's power over death? This study guide will help you glean the deeper meanings and eternal truths woven into C. S. Lewis's tender story of amazing love and salvation.

Scriptures:

Leviticus 4:1–7, 35; Matthew 27:27–55; Matthew 28:1–10; Romans 8:1–4; Ephesians 6:11–18; Hebrews 9:11–10:18.

Based on:

The Lion, the Witch and the Wardrobe, C. S. Lewis (Macmillan Publishing Company, 1950).

PART 1

BOOK SUMMARY: *THE LION, THE WITCH AND THE WARDROBE*

Note to leader: Prior to the class, provide for each person the book, THE LION, THE WITCH AND THE WARDROBE by C. S. Lewis.

Digory, the boy in *The Magician's Nephew,* is now a very old man and famous professor. The tree, that grew from the core of the Narnian apple that saved his mother's life, blew over in a raging storm. Digory, not able to stand the thought of burning the tree as firewood, used the wood for a wardrobe for his home.

Four children, Peter, Susan, Edmund, and Lucy, come to stay with Professor Digory. Lucy hides in the wardrobe during a game of hide and seek. Behind the furs hanging in the wardrobe, Lucy stumbles through a porthole into the magical dimension of Narnia. She discovers Narnia in a state of endless winter under the wicked spell of the White Witch, Jadis. The creatures of Narnia live in constant fear of the White Witch and her cruel wand that gives her the power to transform them into stone.

The White Witch is waiting for human children to enter the land, because she knows of a prophecy that four children will one day rule as kings and queens of Narnia on the four thrones of Cair Paravel. The prophecy also foretells of the witch's death. Lucy is almost betrayed to the White Witch by a faun, named Tumnus. He is convicted of his cowardly motives, however, and subsequently helps Lucy return to her world. Lucy tells her siblings about Narnia, but they do not believe her.

The second time Lucy goes into the wardrobe, Edmund follows her. Edmund does not find Lucy in Narnia, but he does meet the White Witch, Jadis. She tempts him with enchanted Turkish Delight, and Edmund answers all of her questions. After their conversation, Jadis recognizes that these four children are the ones foretold by the prophecy. She persuades Edmund to bring his siblings to her by telling him that when he does this she will give him all the Turkish Delight he wants to eat. Edmund finds Lucy just before they return to their own world. Once they have returned, Edmund does not admit to the older two children that Lucy's story was true, or that he had also been to Narnia.

The third visit to Narnia includes all four children. Due to Edmund's visit with the White Witch, the faun, Tumnus, has been captured by Jadis because he did not follow her orders to turn Lucy over to her. The children set out to rescue Tumnus. They are led by a robin outside of Tumnus' door to the home of beavers who tell them all about the White Witch, the prophecy of the four thrones of Cair Paravel, and Aslan. Upon hearing the beavers' stories, Edmund furtively slips out of the beavers' home. He betrays his siblings to the White Witch because of his lust for Turkish Delight.

The White Witch, Queen Jadis, promptly enslaves Edmund and hunts for the other three children. She intends to stop the prophecy that foretells four sons and daughters of Adam reigning in Narnia. Meanwhile, Aslan, the Creator of Narnia, is moving across the land, and winter is melting into spring. Father Christmas, who had been banned from the land during the endless winter, appears to the children. He provides them with the tools they will need for their future battles, which include a shield, a sword, a bow and a quiver full of arrows, a horn to call for help, a dagger, and a small bottle of cordial for healing.

The White Witch confronts Aslan with the Deep Magic of Narnia that says she has a right to kill Edmund because of his betrayal. Aslan takes Edmund's place and dies on the Stone Table. Lucy and Susan grieve his death through the darkest night of their lives. Near dawn the two sisters hear a tremendous cracking sound. They rush to the table and find it broken in two. Aslan is alive! Aslan tells Susan and Lucy about a deeper magic, from before time began. The deeper magic declares that when a willing and innocent victim is killed in place of a traitor, the table would crack and death would work backwards.

Aslan frees the frozen creatures in the White Witch's castle, and helps Peter who is engaged in battle with the White Witch and her army. Aslan kills the White Witch, and the four children become the queens and kings of Narnia, as predicted in the prophecy before time.

PART 2

DISCOVER THE ETERNAL PRINCIPLES

☛ **Teaching Point One: The lust for sinful pleasures leads to sin and death. Without the shedding of blood there is no forgiveness.**

■ Read Leviticus 4:1–7, 35 and Hebrews 9:11–10:18. "This was enchanted Turkish Delight and anyone who had once tasted it would want more and more of it, and would even, if they were allowed, go on eating it 'till they killed themselves" (Chapter 4). Once Edmund had tasted the enchanted Turkish Delight, his lust and greed for it possessed him, making him a slave to his own desires and controlling his decisions. He wanted Turkish Delight more than he wanted anything else. Eventually his lust led him to the betrayal of his siblings to the White Witch.

Question 1: The White Witch, Jadis, gave Edmund the Turkish Delight. What power did Jadis have over Edmund? Why did she have this power? Could Edmund have escaped her power?

_____

_____

_____

_____

Question 2: What did the Turkish Delight symbolize? How did Edmund's lust for Turkish Delight control his thoughts and actions? Do you think Edmund had the power to control his thoughts? How?

_____

_____

_____

_____

Leader's Note: 2 Corinthians 10:5 says, "We demolish arguments and every pretension that sets itself up against the knowledge of God, and we take captive every thought to make it obedient to Christ." Therefore, we are able to control our thoughts through Christ's strength, grace, and power.

Question 3: "Deep down inside him [Edmund] really knew that the White Witch was bad and cruel" (Chapter 9). Edmund tried to convince himself, however, that she was the rightful queen. Why did Edmund try to deceive himself in this way? What were the results of his self-deception? How does self-deception keep us from accountability for our actions?

_____

_____

_____

_____

_____

_____

As payment for Edmund's sin and betrayal, Jadis demanded Edmund's death on the Stone Table. She believed that if Edmund died, the prophecy of her own death would not be fulfilled. The Deep Magic of Narnia said that Jadis, the White Witch, had a right to kill for every treachery. "His blood is my property," Jadis told Aslan. "[Aslan] knows that unless I have blood as the Law says all Narnia will be overturned and perish in fire and water" (Chapter 13).

C. S. Lewis employed Narnia's Deep Magic as an analogy to the laws and commandments that Moses proclaimed to the people. These laws helped the Israelites to recognize that God was holy. They also made it clear that it was impossible to obey God's laws, which showed them that they were sinful people in need of the Savior.

The animal sacrifices the Levitical law demanded demonstrated the need for the shedding of blood for the forgiveness of sin. They were an annual reminder of sins, and they foretold the sacrificial death of Christ. The animal blood did not take away sins, but it foretold the one and only holy, perfect, and true sacrifice to come—Jesus Christ. Jesus paid the penalty for sin, once and for all, through His shed blood.

Question 4: How does the Deep Magic of Narnia compare and contrast to the Levitical law, given to Moses, which demanded a blood sacrifice for sin?

_____

_____

_____

Question 5: How did the animal sacrifices required in the Levitical law foretell the death of Christ? Why was a blood sacrifice essential for forgiveness? Why did the animals sacrificed need to be without defect?

_____

_____

_____

_____

_____

_____

✐ Leader's Note: Genesis 2:17 and Romans 6:23 tell us that the consequence of sin is death. The animals without defect represented the only holy and perfect sacrifice to come—Jesus Christ.

Question 6: How did the commandments and laws help the Israelites recognize the awesome holiness of God? Do they continue to demonstrate God's holiness today?

_____

_____

_____

_____

Question 7: How did the commandments and laws help the Israelites recognize that they were sinful people? Do the laws and commandments help us recognize our sin today? How does the law help us recognize our need for the Savior?

_____

_____

_____

_____

_____

_____

☛ **Teaching Point Two: Jesus willingly died for our sins.**

■ Read Matthew 27:27–50. Jadis named Edmund a traitor. She claimed he belonged to her, and that she had a right to kill him, because of the Deep Magic. Aslan comforted the frightened and grief-stricken children with these words, "I have settled the matter. She has renounced the claim on your brother's blood."

Jadis renounced the claim on Edmund's blood, because Aslan died in his place. C. S. Lewis used this as a demonstration of how Jesus died for us. Jesus willingly laid down His life to save us from the eternal consequences of our own sins. The tenderness, compassion, and sacrifice of Aslan are the characteristics Jesus demonstrates toward us. He chose to die for us rather than have us be separated from Him for eternity.

Question 8: C. S. Lewis had Aslan die for one boy's sin. How does this symbolize the truth that Jesus died for each of us individually? Does it change your understanding of the crucifixion when you realize Jesus died in your place? Explain your answer.

_____

_____

_____

_____

_____

_____

_____

_____

_____

Question 9: Who does Jadis represent? Why did she believe Edmund belonged to her? What would have happened if Aslan had not died for Edmund? What would happen to us if Jesus had not died for us (consider our life on earth as well as our eternal destiny)?

_____

_____

_____

_____

_____

Leader's Note: Answers should include: We would not have the Holy Spirit to comfort and guide us on earth. We would live in a world of evil, without hope of redemption. The consequences of our sinful lives would consume us. We would face eternal damnation.

The children knew Aslan could have killed his attackers with one swipe of his paw. Instead, he made no noise as they bound him, and he did not resist them in any way. Similarly, Jesus could have called twelve legions of angels to rescue Him (Matthew 26:53). Instead, Jesus did not resist His attackers, defend himself, or answer any of their accusations. "Jesus willingly died and by that will we are made holy through the sacrifice of the body of Jesus once for all" (Hebrews 10:8).

Question 10: Why didn't Jesus resist his attackers? How does it make you feel to realize that Jesus *chose* to die in your place?

_____

_____

_____

Question 11: How does the witch's joy at Aslan's death demonstrate her lack of understanding of the deeper magic that represents God's plan for salvation? What did she think she had won? How was she wrong?

_____

_____

_____

_____

_____

_____

Question 12: Aslan's enemies subjected him to humiliation by shaving his mane. They taunted and jeered at him saying, "He's only a cat after all!" (Chapter 14). How does this compare to the mocking and humiliation of Christ? Why do you think the crowd taunted Jesus? What lack of understanding did this show? What was Christ's response to their taunting and tortures?

_____

_____

_____

_____

☛ **Teaching Point Three: The torn curtain of the temple symbolized that we now have access to God along with the ability to have intimate fellowship with Him.**

■ Read Matthew 27:51–55. In Chapter 15 of *The Lion, the Witch and the Wardrobe,* the Stone Table cracks in two. Susan and Lucy had followed Aslan to the Stone Table and felt the despair and hopelessness of his death. Grieving and numb, they stayed near Aslan's body through the darkest, loneliest night of their lives. At dawn they heard the deafening crack of the Stone Table.

The cracking of the Stone Table symbolizes the tearing of the temple curtain when Jesus died. The curtain separated the Holy Place from the Most Holy Place in the temple. The inner room behind the curtain symbolized God's presence. This inner room was only accessible by the priest. The curtain was a barrier that kept the people from God.

When the curtain was rent from the top to the bottom, it showed that Christ's death allowed access and intimacy with God. The book of Hebrews tells us Jesus entered the Most Holy Place, not of the man-made sanctuary that represented God's presence, but of heaven itself. There He appears for us in God's presence, and His blood gives us eternal life once and for all. We can now have the confidence to enter the holy and magnificent presence of God because of the shed blood of Jesus, our great high priest. We can come to God at any time, any place, and in any circumstance. He is our Abba Father—Daddy God, our most intimate companion and friend, our compassionate and forgiving Savior, as well as the holy and awesome Creator of the universe.

Question 13: Why would this symbolism of the torn curtain be important to the Israelite people? Why do you think there was an earthquake when Jesus died and the curtain tore in two? What was the reaction of those guarding Jesus?

_____

_____

Question 14: How were Susan and Lucy similar to the women in Matthew 27:55? Does reading about Susan and Lucy give you insight into how the women who were near Jesus at the time of his death might have felt? Did anything in particular about the girls' reactions affect you? Share your insights with your group.

_____

_____

_____

_____

_____

_____

Question 15: Why is intimacy with God essential to our spiritual walk? What does it mean to you to know you can have intimacy with God? How do we come into God's presence today?

_____

_____

_____

_____

_____

Question 16: How can you relate to God as your Abba Father, Daddy God? Does it help you to know that God is your perfect parent? Consider the intimacy of a child running into his or her father's arms. How can we run into God's arms? What protection and comfort does God offer us?

_____

_____

_____

_____

_____

_____

_____

_____

_____

_____

_____

Question 17: Does it help you to know that Jesus is your trusted, faithful, and always true friend? If yes, how does this help you? Share an example of a time when you have experienced this.

_____

_____

_____

_____

_____

_____

_____

_____

_____

Question 18: Now that we have access to God, his Holy Spirit is with us at all times, in any place, and in all circumstances. Explain how this brings you peace.

_____

_____

_____

_____

_____

_____

Question 19: Read the section of Chapter 15 where Susan and Lucy romped and played with Aslan. How does this symbolize our intimacy with God?

_____

_____

_____

_____

☛ **Teaching Point Four: Christ's resurrection shows God's victory over death, gives us new life, and enables us to overcome sin.**

■ Read Matthew 28:1–10, Romans 8:1–4, and Ephesians 6:11–18. Christ's death and resurrection give us the power to be set free from the grip sin had on our lives. The book of Romans tells us, "the Spirit of life sets us free from the law of sin and death" (Romans 8:2). Through Christ, we have been set free from the bondage of sin.

The resurrection of Christ proves that He conquered death. Though our physical bodies will one day die, if we belong to Christ, our souls will live with Him eternally. On the day we see Jesus face-to-face, we will be able to proclaim, "Oh Death, where is your victory? Oh Death, where is your sting?" (1 Corinthians 15:55). Death will be the doorway to eternal life.

Aslan told the children that there was a Deeper Magic than the witch knew. This magic was from before time dawned. Aslan told them, "When a willing victim who has committed no treachery was killed in a traitor's stead, the Table would crack and Death itself would start working backwards" (Chapter 15).

Question 20: What do you think the Deeper Magic represents?

_____

_____

_____

✎ *Leader's Note: Answers should include the idea that God's plan before Creation was to send Jesus as Savior to the world. Revelations 13:8 tells us the names of believers were written in the Lamb's book of life before the foundation of the world.*

Question 21: How can death work backwards? How does this compare to 1 Corinthians 15:55 that claims death will have no sting or victory?

_____

_____

_____

_____

_____

_____

Question 22: The book of Romans says Christians are free from the bondage of sin. When Aslan visited the White Witch's castle after his resurrection, he broke the curse of evil that had turned the creatures into statues, and he brought them back to life. What do you think the frozen statues represent? What was symbolized when Aslan broke the spell and brought them back to life? How does their freedom compare to the new life we have in Christ?

_____

_____

_____

_____

_____

_____

_____

_____

_____

_____

Question 23: What does the book of Romans mean, practically, when it says that we are free from the bondage of sin? How can we break the strongholds of sin in our lives?

_____

_____

_____

_____

Question 24: Even though Aslan was brought back to life, the battle with evil continued. Father Christmas gave Peter a shield and a sword and told him that soon he would need to use them. He gave Susan a quiver full of arrows and an ivory horn that she could use to call for help. He gave Lucy a bottle with a cordial for healing and a dagger to defend herself. How does Father Christmas symbolize God's provisions for the spiritual battles we face?

_____

_____

_____

_____

Question 25: Based on Ephesians, what do you think was the symbolism of Peter's sword? How does God's Word help us to fight our spiritual battles? Give practical examples from your own experience. Based on Ephesians, what was the likely symbolism of the shield?

_____

_____

_____

_____

_____

_____

_____

Question 26: Based on Chapter 12, why do you think Aslan told Peter, "Whatever happens, never forget to wipe your sword"? What would be the symbolism of cleaning your sword? Why is it essential for believers to "put on the full armor of God" (Ephesians 6:11)?

_____

_____

_____

_____

_____

_____

_____

_____

_____

_____

Question 27: "Peter did not feel very brave, indeed, he felt like he was going to be sick. But that made no difference to what he had to do" (Chapter 12). Peter fought with the White Witch's wolf and killed him with his sword. How can Satan use our emotions to tempt us to *not do* what God calls us to do in our spiritual battles? Why did C. S. Lewis say Peter's emotions made no difference to what he had to do? Do you agree with this?

_____

_____

_____

_____

_____

_____

_____

_____

PART 3

THE CLOSING CHAPTER

C. S. Lewis explains the love, compassion, and sacrifice of the Savior through this beautifully written story of salvation. Aslan died in the place of Edmund and triumphed over evil. His resurrection demonstrated victory over death. The inability of evil to overcome God's sovereign will is woven throughout this story of the fulfillment of prophecy.

Questions for the Closing Chapter

Question 1: What did you find to be the most powerful passage of this book? Why?

_____

_____

_____

Question 2: Which character did you relate to the most? Why did you relate to him or her?

_____

_____

_____

Question 3: What new thoughts about salvation do you have because you've read this book? What new thoughts about God's great love and sacrifice for you personally have you discovered? What have you learned about God's sovereignty in fulfilling prophecy?

_____

_____

_____

_____

_____

_____

Question 4: What additional themes or messages did you notice in this book?

_____

_____

_____

Optional Activities

▲ *Compare and contrast the crucifixion of Christ with the sacrifice of Aslan.*

■ *Read the crucifixion story in the gospels of Matthew, Mark, Luke, and John. Create a timeline chart from the different gospels.*

Additional Resources

ChristianBibleStudies.com

Beyond the Wardrobe: The Official Guide to Narnia, E. J. Kirk (Zondervan Corp., 2005; ISBN: 0060765534)

Companion to Narnia, Revised Edition, Paul F. Ford (Harpercollins Publishing; ISBN: 0060791276)

Exploring The Lion, the Witch and the Wardrobe, Devin Brown (Baker, 2005; ISBN: 0801065992)

A Field Guide To Narnia, Colin Duriez (Intervarsity Press, 2004; ISBN: 0830832076)

The Heart of Narnia, Thomas Williams (Thomas Nelson/W, 2005; ISBN: 0849904889)

Step Into Narnia: A Journey Through The Lion, the Witch and the Wardrobe (Zondervan Corp., 2005; ISBN: 0060572132)

FULFILLING OUR DESTINY

BOOK: THE HORSE AND HIS BOY

How does Shasta's journey to Narnia to fulfill his destiny
represent God's plan, guidance, and ever-present help in our lives?

C. S. Lewis unfolds a captivating adventure of escape, conspiracy, and royalty in this story about Aslan's sovereign guidance and protection in the lives of two runaway children and their talking Narnian horses. Aslan's greater design for their lives is revealed as the story unwinds to show that they are destined to save Narnia and its close neighbor Archenland from the evil plans of Prince Rabadash. Throughout the plot of this delightful adventure, Lewis demonstrates how God uses the seemingly insignificant and coincidental moments of our lives to guide us to fulfill our destiny.

Unearthing the Deeper Meaning and Truth

How does God guide us through life to fulfill our destiny? What are the purposes of difficulties in our lives? Is there such a thing as luck or coincidence? How can self-conceit lead to insecurity? How does pride steal God's glory? Where is God when I am afraid, hurt, or alone? This study guide will help you to discover the deeper meanings and eternal truths woven into this delightful and humorous story of God's sovereign plan and leading in our lives.

Scriptures:

Exodus 1:22–2:10, 3:1–10; Deuteronomy 8:11–18; Psalm 42; Psalm 46; Proverbs 3:5–6; Philippians 2:3–11.

Based on:

The Horse and His Boy by C. S. Lewis (Scholastic Inc., 1954).

PART 1

BOOK SUMMARY: *THE HORSE AND HIS BOY*

✎ *Note to leader: Prior to the class, provide for each person the book,* THE HORSE AND HIS BOY *by C. S. Lewis.*

A fisherman, who finds an infant in a boat washed ashore from the sea, raises the child, a boy whom he names Shasta. The fisherman is a cruel and abusive father, and as the book begins, Shasta is about to be sold into slavery to a Tarkaan or great lord. The Tarkaan's horse, a talking Narnian horse that had been kidnapped, convinces Shasta to run away with him.

During Shasta and the horse Bree's flight, they meet another horse and rider, Hwin and Aravis. Aravis is a Tarkheena (daughter of a lord) who is escaping her upcoming marriage that was arranged by her hateful stepmother. As they journey along together, they enter the city of Tashbaan where visiting Narnians mistake Shasta for the prince of their neighboring country and ally, Archenland. The prince, Corin, had been traveling with the Narnians in Tashbaan, but he had mysteriously disappeared from their group. Shasta is seized by the Narnians and taken to their queen.

The children from *The Lion, The Witch and The Wardrobe* are now adults and the kings and queens of Narnia. Queen Susan and the others believe Shasta to be the disoriented Prince Corin, therefore they speak openly in front of him. Shasta overhears their plans to escape the city of Tashbaan and the evil prince, Rabadash, who intends to force Queen Susan's hand in marriage.

That evening the real Prince Corin secretly climbs in the window, and Shasta and Corin are stunned to discover that they are mirror images of each other. Meanwhile, through adventures of her own, Aravis overhears Prince Rabadash's plans to capture Queen Susan and attack Archenland and Narnia.

Shasta, Aravis, and the horses begin a race to Archenland and Narnia to relay their information of the coming attack on their lands. They meet dangers along the way, face extreme fatigue, and find the enemy prince and his army constantly on their heels. A lion wounds Aravis, so Shasta continues the journey alone to Archenland. He relays his message in time to allow the armies of Archenland and Narnia to prepare for the pending battle.

The mystery of Prince Corin and Shasta's identical appearance is unraveled when the king of Archenland welcomes Shasta as his long-lost son and Prince Corin's twin. Shasta had been kidnapped as an infant because a jealous spy heard a prophecy that Shasta would save Archenland from a deadly danger. In order to prevent the prophecy from being fulfilled, the spy left him to die at sea, which would surely have happened if the fisherman had not found him. Shasta discovers that he is the heir to the throne of Archenland since he is the older twin, much to Prince Corin's delight.

Aslan meets with Shasta, Aravis, Bree, and Hwin and explains that he was present with them throughout their journey. They recognize that Aslan guided, protected and comforted them as they fulfilled their mission and the prophecy recorded long ago.

PART 2

DISCOVER THE ETERNAL PRINCIPLES

☛ **Teaching Point One: God has a plan for our lives that requires us to trust Him.**

■ Read Exodus 1:22–2:10 and 3:1–10 and Proverbs 3:5–6. Shasta is a Moses-type character.

Aslan's preordained plan to save his people from the evil prince, Rabadash, was interwoven through the tale of a boy rescued from the sea, raised by a cruel fisherman, and destined to save his people. C. S. Lewis showed this when Aslan said to Shasta, "I was the lion." And as Shasta gaped with open mouth and said nothing, he continued, "I was the lion who forced you to join with Aravis. I was the cat who comforted you among the houses of the dead. I was the lion who drove the jackals from you while you slept. I was the lion who gave the horses the new strength of fear for the last mile so that you should reach King Lune in time. And I was the lion you do not remember who pushed the boat in which you lay, a child near death, so that it came to shore where a man sat, wakeful at midnight, to receive you" (Chapter 11).

Kurt Bruner and Jim Ware, in their book *Finding God in the Land of Narnia* (Tyndale House Publishers, 2005), summarize this Providence in Shasta's life. "Had it not been for the fisherman, he would not have fled to Narnia. Had he not fled, he would never have stumbled onto a conspiracy that revealed his place as future king. And had he not been chased by the lion, he would have quit too soon for success. As it turned out, the scenes of Shasta's story he would have preferred to avoid were the ones most important to the larger drama and to his own honored destiny." Bruner and Ware then conclude, "Someday, like Shasta, we will meet the great King and Author of history. Only then will our eyes be opened to the moments in which he was 'the Lion' orchestrating events toward a greater purpose—a greater good. Only then will we better understand how and when the grand drama of providence intersected the smaller scenes of our lives."

God's plans cannot be thwarted (Job 42:2). He weaves circumstances together to lead and guide His children through their lives. Moses was born during a period of oppressive enslavement for the Israelite people. Their lives were bitter with hard labor, and they were told to ruthlessly kill their baby boys. God used even this horrible evil for His glory and the good of His people. The midwives feared God more than they feared man, so they disobeyed Pharaoh's orders and let the boys live. Moses' mother placed him in a basket in the Nile River where Pharaoh's daughter eventually found him and raised him as her own son. This gave Moses the relationship with Pharaoh he needed to free the Israelite people from slavery. God sent Moses to lead the Israelites out of Egypt, and no circumstance could stop that plan. When circumstances in our lives seem out of control, we must trust God instead of leaning on our own understanding. When we acknowledge Him, He promises to guide our paths.

Question 1: Why does the book of Proverbs warn us to not lean on our own understanding? Why do we often struggle with trusting God when we do not understand what He is doing?

_____

_____

_____

_____

_____

"I do think that I must be the most unfortunate boy that ever lived in the whole world. Everything goes right for everyone except me," Shasta said.

After listening to Shasta's laments Aslan responded, "I do not call you unfortunate."

"Don't you think it was bad luck to meet so many lions?" Shasta asked Aslan.

"There was only one lion," Aslan told Shasta. "I was the lion." (Chapter 11)

Question 2: How did Shasta's statement to Aslan show his lack of understanding of Aslan and his ways? How did Aslan's perspective differ from Shasta's perspective? How did C. S. Lewis use this passage to demonstrate that we should trust in the Lord instead of leaning on our own understanding?

_____

_____

_____

_____

_____

Question 3: How did Aslan use the circumstances and difficulties in Shasta's life to guide him to fulfill his destiny? How did Aslan use them to form his character? Give specific examples from the book.

_____

_____

_____

_____

_____

_____

_____

_____

_____

Question 4: Shasta told Bree, "Then we'll go north. I've been longing to go to the North all my life." Why did Shasta's life with the fisherman make him long for the North? Although Shasta didn't know it before he talked to Bree, Narnia lay to the north. What do you think the North represented? How did Shasta's longing for the North, though he knew nothing about it, reveal Aslan's leading in his life?

_____

_____

_____

_____

_____

_____

_____

_____

Question 5: "A day will come when that boy will save Archenland from the deadliest danger in which she ever lay," was the Centaur's prophecy about Cor's (Shasta's) life. How was the prophecy fulfilled? In Chapter 14, how did the enemy, in the form of the Lord Bar, try to prevent the prophecy? How did even this evil plan accomplish Aslan's will?

_____

_____

_____

_____

_____

_____

_____

Question 6: What was Moses' understanding of God's plan (See Exodus 3:11)? How did Moses' understanding differ from God's understanding? How does the story of Moses reveal the truth that God's plans cannot be thwarted?

_____

_____

_____

_____

_____

Question 7: The Israelite midwives feared God more than man, so they did not kill the baby boys. How did the midwives acknowledge God in their decisions to leave the baby boys alive? How did their actions show their trust in God?

_____

_____

_____

_____

_____

_____

_____

Question 8: When the Lord Bar captured the infant Prince Cor he gave him to his knight to "put him out of the way." The knight starved himself to death to keep Prince Cor alive. How did the knight's protection of Cor compare to the midwives' protection of the Israelite babies?

_____

_____

_____

_____

_____

Question 9: The hermit told Aravis that there was no such thing as luck. Then he said, "There is something about all this that I do not understand—but if ever we need to know it, you may be sure that we shall." What does the hermit's statement imply about God revealing His ways to man? Why do you think God allows there to be so much in life that we do not understand?

_____

_____

_____

_____

_____

_____

_____

✎ _**Leader's Note:** Bruner and Ware believe one day, in heaven, we will "better understand how and when the grand drama of providence intersected the smaller scenes of our lives."_

Question 10: How has the Holy Spirit led you through circumstances in your life? Give specific examples. Is it safe to rely solely on circumstances for our guidance? Why or why not?

_____

_____

_____

_____

_____

_____

Leader's Note: Answers should include the ideas that we must first be obedient to God's Word, and we must spend time in prayer seeking God's wisdom.

☛ **Teaching Point Two: God is an ever-present help in times of trouble.**

■ Read Psalm 42 and Psalm 46. "God is good. And that is the problem. He weaves all things toward eventual redemption including the scenes we would rather avoid. He never promised to spare us from hurt or lead us beyond the valley of the shadow of death," say Bruner and Ware in *Finding God in the Land of Narnia.* God is wiser than our pain and perspective. He cares more about our souls than our earthly comforts. There are mysteries in heaven we will never understand on earth. God has promised, however, that whatever we go through, he will be an ever-present help.

Question 11: Review Chapter 6 in *The Horse and His Boy.* When Shasta spent the night alone in the tombs, Aslan was present with him in the form of a cat. How did the cat's presence comfort Shasta? How did Aslan protect Shasta from the jackals? How did this scene portray God's presence in our lives when we are afraid? How does God make His presence known to us in times of trouble? Give specific examples from your own life.

_____

_____

_____

_____

_____

_____

_____

_____

_____

Question 12: In Chapter 11 Aslan walked beside Shasta and eventually spoke to him. As Shasta rode alone to Narnia, he began to cry. He heard breathing beside him and the voice of Aslan said, "Tell me your sorrows." Why is it important to talk to God about our sorrows? How did the author of Psalm 42 express his sorrow to God? What were the Psalmist's conclusions about his troubles?

_____

_____

_____

_____

_____

_____

_____

_____

_____

Question 13: Also in this chapter, Shasta told Aslan, "I can't see you at all." Have you ever experienced a time when you could not feel God's presence? Do you know why? What should we do when we cannot feel God's presence?

_____

_____

_____

_____

_____

_____

Question 14: In Chapter 13 Shasta saw the precipice he had walked in the dark the night before, when Aslan had walked beside him. Shasta had been unaware of his danger. Have you ever experienced a time when God protected you from unknown danger? Share your experience with your group.

_____

_____

_____

_____

_____

Question 15: Aslan scratched Aravis' back to show her the consequences of her unkindness to her stepmother's slave. "You needed to know what it felt like," Aslan told her. How does God often use our pain so that we have compassion for others? Share a time someone has understood your pain because they had walked a similar road.

_____

_____

_____

_____

_____

_____

Question 16: When Shasta told the Narnian creatures of the pending danger, they did not respond quickly because "the smaller woodland people of Narnia were so safe and happy that they were getting a little careless." Do safe and easy times make us careless? What does this statement imply about why God may allow pain in our lives?

_____

_____

_____

_____

_____

☛ **Teaching Point Three: Pride steals God's glory.**

■ Read Deuteronomy 8:11–18 and Philippians 2:3–11. When our heart becomes proud, we forget that God is the one who provides all good things. He provides our strength, talents, opportunities, and anything beneficial in our lives. Pride steals God's glory for ourselves. It seeks to take the credit for everything that God has done in our lives.

The book of Philippians tells us to watch out for the interests of others before we look out for ourselves. When we humble ourselves like this, pride will not lead us to do things out of selfish ambition or vain conceit. Jesus is our model. Though He is God, He thought of our need before His own glory. He humbled himself, became a man, and died in our place.

Pride can make us care more about what others think about us than what God thinks about us. Bree was consumed with what others thought of him. This led to insecurities about his appearance and habits. The least little habit, like rolling in the grass, was analyzed and could become a source of insecurity. Preoccupation with his looks almost kept him from going into Narnia because he was afraid of what the other talking horses would think of him.

Question 17: What are the dangers of caring more about what people think of us than what God thinks of us? How is being a people-pleaser different from looking out for the interests of others? How can being a people-pleaser lead to insecurities? How can insecurities keep us from accomplishing God's will for our lives?

_____

_____

_____

Throughout their journey Bree boasted about being a warhorse and fighting a hundred battles. When the lion chased them, however, Bree did not turn back to help Hwin and Aravis. Shasta had to dismount, while Bree was moving, to go back and fight for his friends. Bree felt humiliated by this after all his bragging, and he considered returning to Calormen and slavery, because he felt he had disgraced himself and lost everything. "My good horse, you've lost nothing but your self-conceit," the Hermit told Bree.

Question 18: How did Bree's bragging set him up to feel disgraced? What did the hermit mean when he said all he had lost was his self-conceit? How does self-conceit steal God's glory?

_____

_____

_____

Question 19: Bree compared himself to the dumb horses that could not talk. This added to his self-conceit and pride. Why is it dangerous to compare yourself with others? How should we evaluate ourselves?

_____

_____

_____

When Bree met Aslan face-to-face, Aslan called him a "poor, proud, frightened horse." Then Aslan told him to draw near to him. "I'm afraid I must be rather a fool," Bree told Aslan. "Happy the horse who knows that while he is still young," was Aslan's reply.

Question 20: Why should being in God's presence humble us so that we see ourselves for who we really are: sinners in need of the Savior? Why did Aslan tell Bree it was good for him to recognize he was a fool?

_____

_____

_____

When Bree remembered how little he knew about Narnia he "got more nervous and more self-conscious with every step he took." As he entered Narnia he "looked more like a horse going to a funeral than a long-lost captive returning to home and freedom."

Question 21: Why was Bree nervous? How can pride rob us of joy?

_____

_____

_____

PART 3

THE CLOSING CHAPTER

C. S. Lewis guides us through a delightful and beautifully told tale of adventures that reveals God's sovereign guidance in the lives of two children and their horses. Through seemingly irrelevant circumstances, coincidences, and the hardships of life, they recognize the hand of God in the form of Aslan leading them to their destiny. Along the path they find God to be their comfort, strength, and counselor as well as their invisible guide.

Questions for the Closing Chapter

Question 1: What portion of the book was most meaningful to you? Why?

_____

_____

_____

Question 2: With which character could you identify the most? Why?

_____

_____

_____

Question 3: What new thoughts about God's sovereign leading did this book reveal to you?

_____

_____

_____

_____

Question 4: Share any areas of conviction or comfort this book gave you.

_____

_____

_____

Question 5: What additional themes or messages did you notice in this book?

_____

_____

_____

Optional Activities

▲ *Compare and contrast the story of Moses with the story of Shasta.*

▲ *Begin a journal of God's leading in your life.*

Additional Resources

ChristianBibleStudies.com

Finding God in the Land of Narnia, Kurt Bruner and Jim Ware (Tyndale House Publishers, 2005; ISBN: 084238104X)

Not a Tame Lion: Unveil NARNIA through the eyes of Lucy, Peter, and other characters created by C. S. Lewis, Bruce L. Edwards (Tyndale House, 2005; ISBN: 1414303815)

The Chronicles of Narnia, Movie Tie-in Edition C. S. Lewis (Zondervan Corp., 2005; ISBN: 0060765453)

The Creatures of Narnia, Scout Driggs (Zondervan Corp., 2005; ISBN: 0060765631)

The World According to Narnia, Jonathan Rogers (Time Warner, 2005; ISBN: 0446696498)

Welcome to Narnia, Jennifer Frantz (Zondervan Corp., 2005; ISBN: 0060765607)

MORE THAN CONQUERORS

BOOK: PRINCE CASPIAN

*We can have joy in the midst of any battle because we know
that we are more than conquerors through Jesus Christ who loves us.*

Aslan's magic draws Peter, Susan, Edmund, and Lucy, whom we met in *The Lion, the Witch and the Wardrobe,* out of their own world and back into Narnia. The children find that the wicked King Miraz has usurped the Narnian throne from his nephew Prince Caspian and has banished all who are known to believe in Aslan, Narnia's creator. Peter, Susan, Edmund, and Lucy assist Prince Caspian in the battle to restore Narnia to its former glory.

Unearthing the Deeper Meaning and Truth

How do we train our children for the battles they will face? How do we respond to the call of God on our lives? Are we willing to follow Christ no matter what the cost? Why should we have hopeful expectation as we wait for God to answer us? How can we have joy in the midst of any battle? This study guide will aid in our understanding of how we can conquer any battle we face in the name of Christ.

Scriptures:

Deuteronomy 6; Isaiah 35; John 21:18–22; Acts 13:45–46, 14:2–7; James 1:22–25; 2 Peter 3:1–9.

Based on:

Prince Caspian by C. S. Lewis (Scholastic Inc., 1951).

PART 1

BOOK SUMMARY: *PRINCE CASPIAN*

✏ *Note to leader: Prior to the class provide for each person the book, PRINCE CASPIAN by C. S. Lewis.*

Aslan's magic draws Peter, Susan, Edmund, and Lucy, the children from *The Lion, The Witch, and The Wardrobe,* back into Narnia. Only a year has passed in the lives of the children while they were in their own world, but hundreds of years have passed in Narnia, so little is familiar to them. They find themselves at the ruins of Cair Paravel where they were once kings and queens of Narnia. A dwarf named Trumpkin finds the children and tells them that Narnia is in great danger. The true heir to the kingdom, Prince Caspian, is being hunted by his uncle, King Miraz, who has usurped the throne. Prince Caspian and all of the Narnian creatures who follow Aslan, the creator of Narnia, are in hiding. In desperation the Narnians had blown the horn of Susan to call Aslan and the children for help. It was this call that had pulled the children into Narnia. Trumpkin had been sent to Cair Paravel to see if the children had arrived and to lead them to Prince Caspian.

Peter, Susan, Edmund, and Lucy must quickly travel to the hideout of the followers of Aslan. However, the children lose a lot of time when they do not follow Aslan when he beckons them. Meanwhile, the creatures of Narnia are growing increasingly impatient because help has not arrived. Some of them decide to take things into their own hands and devise a plan to overthrow the current king. Their plan is rooted in evil, which divides the Old Narnians in their loyalties. Those who have believed faithfully in Aslan continue to expect that he will send help in time, and they refuse to be part of any plans made without Aslan's guidance. Due to the discord, a fight breaks out within the hideout just as help arrives. Those who had devised evil plans are killed in the ensuing struggle leaving only faithful and true Narnians to fight the pending battle with King Miraz.

Since the Narnians faithful to Aslan and Prince Caspian are now even fewer in number, Peter sends a challenge for a dual to King Miraz. He hopes that a dual will prevent an all-out war. The king accepts the challenge. King Miraz falls in the sword fight, and before he can get up, his own men, who have their own secret plans to take over the kingdom, kill him. Those who killed the king blame Peter for the king's death, claiming he stabbed King Miraz in the back. A consequent battle begins between the followers of King Miraz, and the Narnians who are faithful to Aslan and Prince Caspian.

Meanwhile, Aslan has awakened the entire forest of trees, and he and his followers are heading toward the battle in a joyous victory celebration. The trees march into the battle, and King Miraz's men flee to the river where they find the bridge torn down. Since they cannot escape, they throw down their weapons in the presence of Aslan and his joyful followers.

PART 2

DISCOVER THE ETERNAL PRINCIPLES

☛ **Teaching Point One: We must diligently train our children to know, love, trust, and obey God.**

■ Read Deuteronomy 6 and Acts 13:45–46 and 14:2–7. Review chapters 4 and 5 where Prince Caspian learns about Aslan and Old Narnia from the nurse and Dr. Cornelius.

Prince Caspian's nurse diligently told him about Aslan and the old days of Narnia. When the wicked King Miraz discovered this, he banished the faithful nurse from the kingdom. Miraz then proceeded to tell Caspian that all of the stories the nurse had told him were lies and childish nonsense. King Miraz then hired a tutor, Dr. Cornelius, to replace the nurse. Dr. Cornelius, however, covertly continued to tell Caspian the history of Narnia despite knowing that he risked his own life in the process. Eventually Dr. Cornelius helped Caspian escape from the king to save Caspian's life and to protect the throne.

In the book of Deuteronomy, Moses told the Israelites to diligently teach their sons and daughters not to forget God and all he had done for them. He warned them not to follow the false gods of the people who surrounded them. Moses told them to answer their children's questions about God and His laws by telling them about how God had worked in their own lives. When we diligently train our children to love and obey God, we prepare them for the battles they will face in life.

Question 1: Why did the nurse tell Caspian about Aslan and Old Narnia? Knowing Caspian was next in line for the throne, what were her likely hopes and intentions?

_____

_____

_____

Question 2: How did King Miraz react when Prince Caspian spoke of Aslan and Old Narnia? Why did he react this way? What did King Miraz's reaction imply about his spiritual life? Why did King Miraz banish the nurse instead of just reprimanding her and letting her return to her position?

_____

_____

_____

_____

Question 3: Why did Dr. Cornelius continue the stories of Narnia in direct violation of the king's wishes? How was Dr. Cornelius similar to Paul and Barnabas in His boldness?

_____

_____

_____

_____

Question 4: How did the nurse and Dr. Cornelius represent the diligence with which parents should teach their children about God? What specific ways does the book of Deuteronomy say to teach our children? What would this look like today? Why is it important to tell our children how God has worked in our lives personally?

_____

_____

_____

_____

_____

Question 5: The people of Narnia were in danger of forgetting Aslan and Old Narnia. The book of Deuteronomy warns us to not forget God and what He has done for us. Why is it easy to forget what God has done in our lives? What are the results of forgetting?

_____

_____

_____

_____

Question 6: The book of Deuteronomy warns us to not follow the false gods of the people around us. The nurse and Dr. Cornelius' boldly spoke the truth to protect Caspian from the popular but dangerous belief that Aslan did not exist. What are some of the false beliefs of our current culture that we need to warn our children about? How can we protect our children from these lies? Give practical answers.

_____

_____

_____

_____

_____

Question 7: The Jewish people "were filled with jealousy and talked abusively against what Paul was saying" (Acts 13:45), and they "poisoned their minds against the brothers" because they refused to believe (Acts 14:2). How was this situation similar to what King Miraz did to Prince Caspian to counter the nurse's stories?

_____

_____

_____

_____

Question 8: How does diligent training prepare our children for the battles they will face in life?

_____

_____

_____

_____

☞ **Teaching Point Two: We must follow Christ, even if we follow Him alone.**

■ Read John 21:18–22 and James 1:22–25. Review Chapter 9 where Lucy saw Aslan, Chapter 10 where Aslan spoke to Lucy, and Chapter 11 where the other three children finally saw Aslan.

Lucy saw Aslan and knew he wanted her to follow him, but she could not convince the other children that she had seen him. Instead of following Aslan immediately, as she knew Aslan wanted, she followed along behind the other children down the wrong path, weeping as she walked. That path eventually led them into danger. Later Aslan called Lucy away from the group and told her much time had been lost. Lucy blamed her siblings for not believing her, but Aslan told her she should have followed him even if she had to come alone. Aslan gave Lucy a second chance. This time she told her siblings in a tremulous voice, "And I do hope that you will come with me. Because I'll have to go with him whether anyone else does or not" (Chapter 11). Lucy's brothers and sister begrudgingly followed her because they dared not let her wander off alone. In time, each of the other three children began to give up his or her own way of thinking. As their faith increased, they began to see Aslan as Lucy had seen him all along.

Jesus told Peter to follow Him no matter the consequences and not to worry about what John was doing. If Lucy had immediately followed Aslan, she and her siblings would not have experienced the frightening and exhausting consequences of the day. Jesus told us in John 10:27, "My sheep listen to My voice, I know them, and they follow Me." Our response to His call needs to be immediate from a heart willing to trust and obey.

Question 9: Why didn't Lucy follow Aslan the first time? Why did Aslan hold Lucy accountable for not following him, even though she was the youngest? Why didn't Lucy's siblings listen to her? What are the consequences of not following Jesus immediately? Share examples from your own life.

_____

_____

_____

_____

_____

_____

_____

Question 10: When Edmund asked Lucy how she knew Aslan wanted them to follow him, Lucy replied, "He...I...I just know by his face." How does this line speak of Lucy's intimacy with Aslan? How do we know what God wants us to do? How can other people dissuade us from what God calls us to do?

_____

_____

_____

_____

_____

_____

_____

Question 11: It was not until Lucy told her siblings she would follow Aslan by herself if she had to that they decided to follow her. How does our obedience or disobedience to God affect other people? Have you ever had to take a stand for Christ alone as Lucy did for Aslan? What were the results of your decision?

_____

_____

_____

_____

_____

_____

_____

Question 12: Why couldn't the other children see Aslan right away? Why did he start to become visible as they followed Lucy? Have you ever had to step out in faith before God revealed himself to you? If yes, share your experience with the group.

_____

_____

_____

_____

_____

_____

_____

Question 13: Susan told Lucy, "I really believed it was him...he, I mean...yesterday. When he warned us not to go down to the fir-wood. And I really believed it was him tonight, when you woke us up. I mean, deep down inside. Or I could have, if I'd let myself. But I just wanted to get out of the woods and...and...oh, I don't know; and what ever am I to say to him?" (Chapter 11). The book of James tells us that if we only listen to the Word of God and do not obey it, we deceive ourselves. How did Susan deceive herself? What does God promise to those who do not only hear God's Word but choose to obey it (James 1:25)? Susan wondered aloud what she should say to Aslan. What should we say to God when we recognize our disobedience?

_____

_____

_____

_____

Question 14: Aslan had Lucy, the youngest, lead the way. "The others had only Lucy's directions to guide them, for Aslan was not only invisible to them but silent as well" (Chapter 11). Why do you think Lucy could see Aslan when the others couldn't see him? Why do you suppose Aslan chose Lucy to lead the group?

_____

_____

_____

_____

_____

_____

_____

Question 15: Jesus told us to come to Him with the faith of a child (Matthew 18:3). What did Jesus mean when He said that we must become like little children? How did the more adult reasoning of the older children actually hinder their faith? Have you ever experienced a time when a child's faith was stronger than your own? Share your experience with your group.

_____

_____

_____

_____

_____

Question 16: "Lucy had her eyes on the lion and the rest had their eyes on Lucy" (Chapter 11). How can we help lead others to Christ when we keep our eyes focused on Jesus?

_____

_____

_____

Question 17: One of the verses of the hymn _I Have Decided to Follow Jesus_ says, "Though none go with me, still I will follow—no turning back." Why is it important to decide that we will follow Jesus, even if we must follow alone? Why is it important to have this resolution before we face a situation like Lucy did?

_____

_____

_____

_____

_____

_____

_____

_____

☛ **Teaching Point Three: Wait for the Lord.**

■ Read 2 Peter 3:1–9. Review Chapter 12 in the book.

Prince Caspian and his followers blew Susan's horn that was promised to summon help. Help did not come immediately, however, and some of the members of Caspian's group gave up hope. They were ready to turn to their own evil devices to win the pending battle.

The book of Peter warns us that scoffers will come questioning why God has not fulfilled His promise to return to earth. It tells us these people "deliberately forgot" all God had told them. We must not forget that God is not on our time schedule, for to Him "a thousand years are like a day." What we often interpret as slowness is actually God's patience as He waits for the perfect time to fulfill His plans. As David waited on the Lord, he spoke of his confidence—knowing that he would see God's goodness (Psalm 27:13). Let us not be discouraged when we have times of waiting, but instead may our attitude be one of hopeful expectation that relies on His promises as truth.

Question 18: "Are you still asking us to hang our hopes on Aslan and King Peter and all the rest of it?" Nikabrik asked Prince Caspian and Dr. Cornelius (Chapter 12). Dr. Cornelius then confessed that he, too, was deeply disappointed in the apparent lack of results that came from blowing Susan's horn. Why do you think God sometimes chooses not to respond immediately or in a way we want or expect Him to respond?

_____

_____

_____

Question 19: Nikabrik devised his own scheme that included the very evil they were fighting against. Why are we tempted to come up with our own plans when we are waiting for God to act? If we are walking with Christ, how can waiting actually deepen our intimacy with God and strengthen our faith?

_____

_____

_____

_____

Question 20: How did Nikabrik use the fatigue and fears of Prince Caspian's band to try to convince them to give up their hope in Aslan's help? How does Satan do this with us? How can we use God's Word as a sword of truth to combat the enemy's lies?

_____

_____

_____

_____

Question 21: "The help will come," said Trufflehunter. "I stand by Aslan. Have patience, like us beasts. The help will come. It may be even now at the door." "Best of badgers," King Peter said to Trufflehunter, "You never doubted us all through" (Chapter 12). How did Trufflehunter's faith compare to what the book of Peter said about waiting for God to fulfill His promises?

_____

_____

_____

Question 22: Prince Caspian said Nikabrik "had gone sour inside from long suffering and hating" (Chapter 12). If we do not rely on God with expectant hope, we can become bitter during times of difficulty. What are the consequences of bitterness? How do we, by God's strength, fight against bitterness?

_____

_____

_____

_____

_____

_____

☛ **Teaching Point Four: We have joy in God's presence for we know He has won the victory over sin, and we are more than conquerors in Him.**

■ Read Isaiah 35. Review Chapter 14 where Aslan leads the joyful victory celebration.

Aslan began the victory celebration while the battle over Narnia was still raging. Those who loved Aslan were intoxicated by the joy of his presence and the hope of victory in his name. The trees and river were set free to join in the festive march, and joy permeated the air with leaping, dancing, singing, music, and laughter.

Whatever battles we face, we know we are more than conquerors through Christ who loves us (Romans 8:37). We can have joy in any battle we face because of the hope of victory in His name. Whatever God allows in our lives He will use for our good and His glory. The enemy has already been defeated—in this we have joy.

One day everlasting joy will crown our heads, and we will enter Zion with gladness and singing. The land and wilderness will be vibrant and beautiful and will rejoice greatly with shouts of praise. The waters will gush forth in a land once dry and desert. The lame will leap for joy, the blind will see, the deaf will hear, and the mute will shout their praise. Our joy will be complete when we, the ransomed of the Lord, enter Zion with singing (Isaiah 51:11).

Question 23: How did Aslan's romp portray our hope of victory through Christ in any battle we face? What was the significance of the celebration beginning before the war had ended?

_____

_____

_____

_____

_____

Question 24: Why did most people run away from Aslan and his victory parade? What did the few people who joined Aslan represent?

_____

_____

_____

_____

When Aslan entered the cottage of the dying woman, who had been Caspian's nurse, she cried with joy, "Oh, Aslan! I knew it was true. I've been waiting for this all my life. Have you come to take me away" (Chapter 14)?

Question 25: For what had the woman been waiting her entire life? In what was her joy and hope rooted? The day we meet our Savior face-to-face will be our ultimate victory day. Why should this give us great joy? Share with your group thoughts that you have about the day you will see Jesus face-to-face.

_____

_____

_____

_____

_____

Question 26: How does the dance of the trees and the freeing of the river in _Prince Caspian_ compare to Isaiah 35?

_____

_____

_____

Question 27: The book of Isaiah tells us to take courage and be strong in the hope of His coming. How does looking forward to His coming and the joy of eternity give us courage and strength to face our daily battles?

_____

_____

_____

_____

PART 3

THE CLOSING CHAPTER

The Old Narnians found that they were more than conquerors with the strength and help of Aslan. They learned to keep their eyes focused on him and to hope expectantly for his rescue. They were consumed with joy in his presence, knowing he would be victorious.

Questions for the Closing Chapter

Question 1: What did you find to be the most meaningful passage of this book? Why?

_____

_____

_____

Question 2: To which character could you relate the most? Why? For which character did you feel empathy? Which character(s) made you angry? Explain your reactions to these characters.

_____

_____

_____

_____

Question 3: What new thoughts or insights about God do you have because you read this book?

_____

_____

_____

_____

Optional Activities

▲ *Aslan lead the Old Narnians back to Narnia in a victory march similar to the return of the redeemed to Zion found in Isaiah. Compare and contrast the return of the redeemed in Isaiah 35 to Aslan's joyous celebration.*

▲ *Develop a plan to help you diligently train your children to love and obey God. Have at least three specific ideas to assist you in this endeavor.*

Additional Resources

ChristianBibleStudies.com

Beyond The Wardrobe: The Official Guide to Narnia, E. J. Kirk (Zondervan Corp., 2005; ISBN: 0060765534)

Companion to Narnia, Revised Edition, Paul F. Ford (Harpercollins Publishing; ISBN: 0060791276)

Exploring The Lion, The Witch And The Wardrobe, Devin Brown (Baker, 2005; ISBN: 0801065992)

A Field Guide To Narnia, Colin Duriez (Intervarsity Press, 2004; ISBN: 0830832076)

The Heart of Narnia, Thomas Williams (Thomas Nelson/W, 2005; ISBN: 0849904889)

Step Into Narnia: A Journey Through The Lion, The Witch and the Wardrobe (Zondervan Corp., 2005; ISBN: 0060572132)

A HEART SET ON ETERNITY

BOOK: THE VOYAGE OF THE DAWN TREADER

How does a heart set on eternity influence the way we live each day?

In this inspiring adventure on the high seas of Narnia and the islands encountered along the way, C. S. Lewis unfolds a story of character and courage as the crew of the ship *Dawn Treader* learns to keep its focus on eternity. Cruel slave traders, violent storms, fire-breathing dragons, enchanted waters, and mythical sea creatures abound throughout their magical journey. The crew of the *Dawn Treader* also struggles with inner battles of the soul including selfishness, greed, and fear. When the people find their strength, hope, and help in Aslan, the creator of Narnia, these temptations eventually develop their character and strengthen their faith. C. S. Lewis reminds us to keep our focus on eternity and to fight our battles utilizing the strength and grace of God.

Unearthing the Deeper Meaning and Truth

What would we look like if our outward appearance reflected our inner character? Why must we rely on God's power to change our lives? What are the various forms of greed, and how do they affect our choices and character? What are the consequences of fear? How does a focus on eternity affect our daily lives? This study guide will help you harvest the pearls of wisdom C. S. Lewis laced into this magical adventure of the sea.

Scriptures:

Psalm 27:1–3; Ecclesiastics 3:11–12; Isaiah 51:12–15; Luke 12:13–34; John 4:10–15; Romans 7:15–25; 2 Corinthians 4:14–18; Revelations 3:4–5, 7:9–17.

Based on:

The Voyage of the DAWN TREADER by C. S. Lewis (Scholastic Inc., 1952).

PART 1

BOOK SUMMARY: *THE VOYAGE OF THE DAWN TREADER*

✐ *Note to leader: Prior to the class, provide for each person the book,* THE VOYAGE OF THE DAWN TREADER *by C. S. Lewis.*

Lucy and Edmund, the younger children from *The Lion, the Witch and the Wardrobe,* are visiting their obnoxious cousin, Eustace, while their parents vacation in America. While looking at a picture of a ship that reminds Edmund and Lucy of the grand and royal ships they had sailed in their previous trips to Narnia, the picture comes to life and all three of the surprised children are swept off their feet by a huge wave which draws them down into a cold, wind-tossed, salt sea. They are rescued by the people of the *Dawn Treader,* the ship from the picture. Caspian, the prince from the book, *Prince Caspian,* is now the king of Narnia. He is sailing to find and rescue seven lords of Narnia who, during his wicked uncle's reign, had been banished to sea because they were loyal to Prince Caspian and Aslan, the creator of Narnia.

The crew of the *Dawn Treader* undergoes an adventurous journey across mythical seas and enchanted islands. Eventually, they find all seven of the lost lords and arrive at the last magical sea at the end of the world. Each island holds an intriguing adventure of its own, and eternal truths are learned along the exhilarating voyage. During their adventures, the children face brutal storms, fearsome dragons, mystical sea creatures, faith-testing temptations, and inner character struggles. Throughout their sea-faring adventure they learn much about the faithfulness and loving kindness of Aslan, as well as the joys and hopes of eternity.

On the first island, evil slave traders who have overrun the island with the permission of the wicked Governor Gumpas capture the children. With the help of the first of the seven lords, Lord Bern, they restore the island to Narnian control, release the slaves from captivity, and make Lord Bern the Duke of the island.

On Dragon Island, Eustace, who is known for bad character and selfish behavior, becomes a dragon that represents his inner character. Aslan helps him return to the form of a boy, and Eustace's character is transformed. The children discover that the second of the lords, Lord Octesian, met his death on this island either by being killed by a dragon or turning into a dragon.

The third island they visit has a pond that turns everything that touches its enchanted water into gold. Enticing greed nearly overcomes the bedazzled children until Aslan appears, and his presence breaks the cursed spell of insatiability that has come upon them. They name the island Deathwater Island because they have found the third lord turned into a golden statue at the bottom of the enchanted pool.

On the Island of Voices, the children come upon a group of invisible and foolish inhabitants who need Lucy to break their enchantment by reading from a book of spells. The inhabitants, named Dufflepuds, lack courage and wisdom to break the spell themselves. Lucy struggles with her own courage and temptations as she reads through the mysterious book. Aslan meets her between the pages of the book, the spell is broken, and the inhabitants are free from the curse of being invisible.

Near the Dark Island, the children sail in eerie, absolute darkness that is seemingly impenetrable by light. They find a terrified and panicked stranger in the black mysterious water. He is the fourth of the seven lost lords, Lord Rhoop. He has nearly lost his sanity from fear. The fear is contagious and soon the children find themselves nearing nightmarish despair. Reepicheep, the mouse, alone is courageous and recognizes that the members of the crew are in a panic. Lucy desperately calls on Aslan who delivers them from the darkness, and more importantly, from their overwhelming, nameless fear.

The island, at the end of the world, contains three men in an enchanted, timeless sleep. They are the last of the seven lords. To break the spell they are under, a volunteer must sail to the end of the world and never return. Aslan's land is at the end of the world, so Reepicheep, who has always longed for Aslan's land, volunteers for the job. The *Dawn Treader* sails to the end of the world where they encounter a heaven-like sea. Reepicheep, the mouse, sails alone from there to Aslan's country while Edmund, Lucy, and the reformed Eustace return to their own world.

PART 2

DISCOVER THE ETERNAL PRINCIPLES

☛ **Teaching Point One: If any man is in Christ he is a new creation.**

■ Read Romans 7:15–25 and Revelations 3:4–5, 7:9–17. Review Chapters 6 and 7 in *The Voyage of the Dawn Treader.*

Bad character and self-centeredness engulfed Eustace. His journal showed that he had even deceived himself into believing the lies that he used to justify his behavior. When Eustace turned into a dragon, his outward appearance symbolized his inner man. Eustace first had to recognize and admit who he was before he could change. Once Eustace recognized that he was a dragon, which was symbolic of his sinful nature, he desired to change not only his outward appearance, but his inner character as well. He tried to peel off his dragon skin, but each time he thought it was removed, he found another dragon skin underneath. Aslan was the only one who could permanently remove Eustace's dragon skin. After Aslan removed the skin, he threw Eustace into a pond and then took him out and dressed him in new clothes.

In the book of Romans, the apostle Paul openly and honestly shared his struggle with sin. He recognized his inability to change in his own power. With a heart of praise, Paul glorified Jesus for rescuing him from the power of sin in his life. Only Jesus can give us the power to overcome sin and change our behavior so that we become more like Christ. The Book of Revelation tells us that those whose names are written in the Lamb's Book of Life will one day be clothed in white robes. Our raiment will represent the righteousness imputed to us by grace through faith in the blood of Christ.

Question 1: "Sleeping on a dragon hoard with greedy, dragonish thoughts in his heart, he had become a dragon himself" (Chapter 6). How did the dragon symbolize Eustace's sinful nature? How did being a dragon help Eustace to recognize his sinful nature? How did it make him desire to change, not only his outward appearance, but his inner character as well? Why is the first step to repentance agreement with God that we are sinful?

_____

_____

_____

_____

_____

_____

_____

_____

_____

Question 2: Why did Eustace find another dragon skin underneath each layer that he peeled off? How does this compare to the passage in the book of Romans where Paul talks about his struggle with the sinful nature? Why was Aslan the only one who could remove Eustace's dragon skin permanently?

_____

_____

_____

_____

_____

_____

_____

Question 3: Why did it hurt Eustace when Aslan removed his dragon skin? Is there pain involved when we give up our sinful habits? Explain your answer. Why didn't it hurt when Eustace tried to peel off his own skin? Why was the skin Aslan took off Eustace "ever so much thicker, and darker, and more knobbly-looking than the others had been" (Chapter 7)?

_____

_____

_____

_____

_____

_____

_____

Question 4: What did the new clothes Aslan put on Eustace represent? 1 Peter 5:5 instructs us to be clothed with humility. What other character qualities might be represented by the new clothes which Aslan gave Eustace?

_____

_____

_____

_____

Question 5: What did the water represent that Aslan threw Eustace into once his dragon skin was peeled off? Eustace said the water "smarted like anything but only for a moment. After that it became perfectly delicious, and as soon as I started swimming and splashing I found that all the pain had gone from my arm" (Chapter 7). Why is it painful to give up our old nature? How is new life in Christ "perfectly delicious"? How does Christ heal the pain caused by our sin nature?

_____

_____

_____

_____

_____

_____

✐ *Leader's Note: The water could symbolize baptism, which represents our old self being buried with Christ and our new self raised to walk in a new life (Romans 6:4).*

Question 6: Lewis said, "It would be nice, and fairly nearly true, to say that 'from that time forth Eustace was a different boy.' To be strictly accurate, he began to be a different boy. He had relapses. There were still many days when he could be very tiresome. But most of those I shall not notice. The cure had begun" (Chapter 7). What was the cure? Why do Christians continue to struggle with sin? When will our struggle with sin cease, as explained by Paul in the Book of Romans?

_____

_____

_____

_____

_____

_____

Leader's Note: Although Christ forgave our sins on the cross, we still battle our evil natures. Our struggle with sin will only end at our death or the return of Christ.

☛ **Teaching Point Two: Be on your guard against every form of greed.**

■ Read Luke 12:13–34. Throughout the *Dawn Treader's* voyage, greed affects the thoughts, motives, and choices of C. S. Lewis's characters. In each situation Lewis portrayed the enticement and potential consequences of greed.

In the book of Luke, Jesus warned His followers to be on guard against every form of greed. Life does not consist of what we own, and we never know when God will require our soul. Jesus warned us to lay up our treasures in heaven, not on earth. He is our great provider, and He will take care of our needs. God calls us to give generously and without compunction from purses that do not wear out, for where our treasure is, there our heart will be, also.

■ Read Chapter 9 where Prince Caspian, Eustace, Lucy, Edmond and Reepicheep explore Deathwater Island.

The *Dawn Treader* beached on a small desolate island. The children and Reepicheep happened upon a pool with a golden statue at the bottom. When Edmund checked the depth of the pool with his spear, it turned to gold. The search party then realized the statue at the bottom of the pool had once been a man, and that whatever touched the mystical water of the pond would turn to gold. Greed began to capture the thoughts and intentions of the boys, and they began to quarrel over who was the king and who owned the island. When Aslan suddenly appeared in the distance, however, "they looked at one another like people waking from sleep" (Chapter 8).

Question 7: "'The king who owned this island,' said Caspian slowly and his face flushed as he spoke, 'would soon be the richest of all kings of the world'" (Chapter 8). What effect did the thought of being the richest king in the world have on Caspian? Why?

_____

_____

_____

The book of Luke relates a similar story. "Tell my brother to divide the inheritance with me," someone in the crowd had called to Jesus. Jesus responded, "Watch out! Be on your guard against all kinds of greed"(Luke 12:15).

Question 8: Why did Jesus warn us to "Watch out!" for greed? How did greed sneak up suddenly on Prince Caspian? How can greed sneak up on us? What forms can greed take?

_____

_____

_____

_____

_____

Question 9: Why did Aslan's presence help the children realize they were in danger of greed controlling their thoughts, motives, and actions? Why is it essential to ask God for wisdom with finances and material possessions?

_____

_____

_____

Question 10: Jesus said, "A man's life does not consist in the abundance of his possessions" (Luke 12:15). What did Jesus mean by this statement? Our culture often measures a man's worth by his possessions. Why is it essential to remember that all of our possessions belong to God? Is it possible to possess many things and not be greedy? How can we share what we have with others on a daily basis?

_____

_____

_____

_____

📖 *Leader's Note: Possible answers include hospitality, transportation, housing, and caring for those in need locally and overseas.*

Question 11: In Chapter 4 of the text, Caspian asked Governor Gumpas why he had allowed slavery. Gumpas replied that it was "an essential part of the economic development of the islands, I assure you. Our present burst of prosperity depends on it." How can greed lead us to make choices that hurt other people? How did this same thought process about slavery damage our nation? What long-term consequences of slavery still exist today? How can focusing on our "present burst of prosperity" negatively influence our long-term choices?

_____

_____

_____

_____

_____

_____

_____

_____

_____

_____

Question 12: In Luke 12 God called the rich man a fool. How was he foolish? How can we be rich toward God?

_____

_____

_____

📖 **Teaching Point Three: We do not need to fear, for God is our refuge and strength, and He is with us wherever we go.**

■ Read Isaiah 51:12–15 and Psalm 27:1–3. Read Chapter 12 in the text.

Thick, deep darkness engulfed the *Dawn Treader*. Nothing could be seen. Light from the lanterns would not permeate the black waters. Suddenly there was a cry of extreme terror from someone who had nearly lost his sanity. A white face with wild expression appeared in the light of the lantern, revealing an expression filled with "the agony of pure fear."

"Fly! Fly! About with your ship and fly! Row, row, row for your lives away from this accursed shore," the stranger cried in desperation once he had been rescued from the black waters

64

(Chapter 12). The stranger explained that they were near an island where dreams—horrible nightmarish dreams—come true. His obsessive fear gripped the crew of the *Dawn Treader* and the crew began to sink in the quicksand of terror. Only Reepicheep, the mouse, recognized what was happening. "This is a panic, this is a rout," he exclaimed (Chapter 12). Caspian retorted, "There are some things no man can face"(Chapter 12). Nightmarish imagination fueled by petrifying fear gripped the souls of the sailors. Lucy cried out to the one she loved best, "Aslan, Aslan, if ever you loved us at all, send us help now." Suddenly Lucy began to feel better and she realized, "After all, nothing has really happened to us yet" (Chapter 12).

Many times throughout the Bible, God tells us not to be afraid. Fear wraps its tentacles around our soul and chokes our faith. Faith and fear are polar opposites. If we are strong in faith, we will not fear. If we are weak in faith, fear will control us. We do not need to fear the future for God is already there. We do not need to fear circumstances for God is our Maker and is in control of all things. If we live in fear, we forget our Maker who is all-powerful and whose sovereignty works all things for His glory and our good.

Question 13: Of what was the stranger in the sea afraid? How did his fear affect him? Consider the physical, emotional and spiritual effects fear had on him. Why was the stranger's fear contagious? What part did imagination have in the fear of the crew of the *Dawn Treader*?

_____

_____

_____

_____

_____

_____

Question 14: Do you agree with Caspian that "there are some things no man can face"? How does this compare to Joshua 1:9 that says, "Be strong and courageous. Do not be terrified; do not be discouraged, for the Lord your God will be with you wherever you go"? Is there ever a healthy fear that keeps us from danger?

_____

_____

_____

_____

_____

_____

_____

Question 15: Isaiah 41:10 says, "Do not anxiously look about you, for I am your God. I will strengthen you, surely I will help you, surely I will uphold you with My righteous right hand"(NASB). How was the crew of the *Dawn Treader* "anxiously looking about them"? What did this do to their faith? How did the crew of the *Dawn Treader* anxiously look at the stranger and fear for themselves? Have you ever heard of a tragedy and been afraid it would happen to you? Share your experience with your group. Why does God tell us to not anxiously look about us?

_____

_____

_____

_____

_____

_____

_____

_____

_____

_____

_____

_____

Question 16: "Only Reepicheep remained unmoved." God calls us to "stand firm. Let nothing move you. Always give yourselves fully to the work of the Lord" (1 Corinthians 15:58). What does it mean to be immoveable? How did Reepicheep portray the steadfastness described in this passage?

_____

_____

_____

_____

Question 17: Reepicheep said, "No danger seems to me so great as that of knowing when I get back to Narnia that I left a mystery behind me through fear" (Chapter 13). What would have happened if the children had let fear keep them from entering the unknown darkness? How can fear keep us from accomplishing God's work in our lives?

_____

_____

_____

_____

Question 18: David said in Psalm 56:4, "When I am afraid, I will trust in You." How did Lucy's response when she called on Aslan compare to David's response? Is it wrong to have the emotion of fear? When we feel the emotion of fear, what should be our response?

_____

_____

_____

_____

Question 19: After Lucy called on Aslan, she felt better, even though the darkness had not diminished. Why did she feel better even though her circumstances had not changed? What were the eventual results of Lucy calling on Aslan?

_____

_____

_____

_____

Question 20: What was the symbolism of the albatross first looking like a cross? The albatross whispered to Lucy, "Courage, dear heart." God spoke similarly to Joshua when He told him to be strong and courageous (Joshua 1:9). What is courage? Why is courage essential to our faith?

_____

_____

Question 21: Aslan destroyed the darkness. What did the darkness represent? Share an experience where God destroyed darkness in your life.

_____

_____

_____

_____

_____

_____

☛ **Teaching Point Four: We must keep our eyes on eternity.**

■ Read Ecclesiastics 3:11–12, 2 Corinthians 4:14–18, and John 4:10–15. Read Chapter 15 in the text.

Reepicheep had eternity set in his heart. "I expect to find Aslan's own country," he said. "I do not know what it means. But the spell of it has been on me all my life" (Chapter 2). Reepicheep's desire to be with Aslan permeated his life so that his character was honorable and courageous. He desired to be in Aslan's land more than he desired anything else.

God has set eternity in our hearts. When our focus is God's eternal kingdom, we realize everything on earth is temporal. This allows us to see beyond the trappings of this life. Material possessions lose their grip on us. Pain and sorrow are reduced because of the joy set before us. Decisions and choices are based on eternal values. Our focus becomes one of pleasing Christ and accomplishing His work here on earth. With eternity as our focal point, we can rejoice and do good in our lifetime, knowing everything good is a gift from God.

Question 22: "My own plans are made. While I can, I sail east in the *Dawn Treader*. When she fails me, I paddle east in my coracle. When she sinks, I shall swim east with my four paws. And when I can swim no longer, if I have not reached Aslan's country, I shall sink with my nose to the sunrise and Peepiceek will be head of the talking mice in Narnia" (Chapter 14). How did Reepicheep's eternal perspective affect his life? How should an eternal perspective comfort us? How should an eternal perspective affect our life's decisions and choices?

_____

_____

_____

_____

_____

_____

Question 23: As the children journeyed to the end of the world where Reepicheep would go on to Aslan's country, there was a sea that contained water with mythical characteristics. Old men became younger. The crew had renewed joy and excitement. They no longer felt tired. The vision of all who drank from the sea improved. Similarly, Jesus told the woman at the well that He would give her living water so that she would never be thirsty again (John 4:10). What is the living water Jesus is talking about? How did the sea before Aslan's land compare to or contrast with the "living water" or the "water of life" that Jesus offers to us?

_____

_____

_____

_____

_____

✒ *Leader's Note:* *The Book of Revelation tells us that in eternity the Lamb will lead us to springs of living water, and we will never again be hungry or thirsty. The sun will not scorch us. God will wipe every tear from our eyes (Revelation 7:16–17).*

Question 24: Caspian asked Drinian what he saw ahead of the ship. "I see whiteness. All along the horizon from north to south, as far as my eyes can see," was the reply. The whiteness was touched with gold. What is the likely symbolism of the white and gold that lay ahead of the crew as they gazed toward Aslan's land?

_____

_____

_____

_____

✒ *Leader's Note:* *White stands for purity, holiness, and light of Christ. Gold stands for majesty.*

Question 25: A lamb met the children near Aslan's land and told them they must enter Aslan's country from their own world. He told them their way lay across a river but that he was the great bridge builder. Who did the lamb represent? How is Jesus our great bridge-builder?

_____

_____

_____

_____

_____

_____

PART 3

THE CLOSING CHAPTER

The crew of the *Dawn Treader* learned to keep their eyes on eternity in this adventurous and humorous tale of the high seas of Narnia and their enchanted islands. C. S. Lewis's characters developed inner strength and increased faith throughout their journey to the end of the world. Lewis gave us a glimpse into heaven as Reepicheep traveled into Aslan's land.

Questions for the Closing Chapter

Question 1: At the end of the story Aslan, in the form of a lamb, told the children that they must return to their own world, and that the reason for their coming to Narnia was so "that by knowing me here for a little, you may know me better there"(Chapter 15). What does this statement tell us about C. S. Lewis's purpose for *"The Chronicles of Narnia"*? How has this book helped you learn more about God?

_____

_____

_____

_____

_____

_____

Question 2: What did you find to be the most powerful passage of this book?

_____

Question 3: Which character did you relate to the most? Why did you relate to him or her?

_____

_____

_____

Question 4: What new thoughts about eternity do you have because you read this book?

_____

_____

_____

Question 5: What additional themes or messages did you notice in this book?

_____

_____

_____

_____

_____

_____

⬜ *Optional Activities*

▲ *Compare or contrast the last sea and the end of the world in* The Voyage of the Dawn Treader *to what the book of Revelation says about eternity.*

▲ Memorize verses from the Bible that call you to courage.

Additional Resources

ChristianBibleStudies.com

Freedom from Fear Overcoming Worry and Anxiety, Neil Anderson (Harvest House Publishers, 1999; ISBN: 0736900721)

Heaven, Randy Alcorn (Tyndale House, 2004; ISBN: 0842379428)

Money and Possessions, Kay Arthur & David Arthur (Random House, Inc., 2004; ISBN: 1578569060)

Money Possessions and Eternity, Revised and Updated, Randy Alcorn (Tyndale House, 2003; ISBN: 0842353607)

Someday Heaven, Larry Libby (Zondervan Corp., 2001; ISBN: 0310701058)

Straight Talk on Fear, Joyce Meyer (Time Warner Book Group, 2003; ISBN: 0446691526)

VICTORIOUS RESCUE

BOOK: THE SILVER CHAIR

*Why should the hope of resurrection give us
the power to live life boldly for the sake of Christ?*

This captivating tale revolves around the search and rescue of a prince from the clutches of the evil underworld. C. S. Lewis intertwines the biblical truth that for Christians "to live is Christ and to die is gain" (Philippians 1:21). Eustace, Jill, and their guide, Puddleglum, discover the importance of following Aslan's directions no matter what the circumstance or cost. They find courage to fight their enemies because they know Aslan will be with them whether they live or die. When King Caspian dies, Aslan rescues him from the power of death through resurrection victory. Lewis illustrates Christ's victory over death and the hope and joy of the resurrected body and life everlasting.

Unearthing the Deeper Meaning and Truth

Why is it essential to meditate on God's Word? Why must we be willing to follow Christ regardless of the circumstance or cost? Does God promise to keep us safe? Why is physical death the final victory for a believer? This study will help us discern the eternal truths and symbolisms C. S. Lewis embedded in this story of faith in the face of imminent danger.

Scriptures:

Psalm 119:92–104; Isaiah 35:5–6; Daniel 3:13–18; 1 Corinthians 15:35–55; Philippians 1:12–30; Hebrews 2:15; James 1:22–25.

Based on:

The Silver Chair by C. S. Lewis (Scholastic Inc., 1953).

Part 1

Book Summary: *The Silver Chair*

📝 *Note to leader: Prior to the class, provide for each person the book, THE SILVER CHAIR by C. S. Lewis.*

Eustace, the boy who turned into a dragon in *The Voyage of the DAWN TREADER*, meets a young girl at school named Jill Pole. While Eustace and Jill are escaping from school bullies, they run through a door in a garden wall and find themselves in Narnia. Aslan sends them on a mission to rescue Prince Rilian, who has been captured by an evil queen. Aslan gives Jill four signs to aid them in their journey to find the prince, impressing upon her the importance of memorizing and remembering these signs.

Eustace and Jill are joined by a Marsh-wiggle named Puddleglum. Puddleglum is a frog/man creature who acts as their guide. All along the way the three travelers face obstacles, hardships, and discomforts. As the search party becomes tired and weak, they begin to forget about the four signs, in spite of Puddleglum's encouragement to repeat them.

To avoid being captured by pursuing giants, the search party escapes into a cave, which leads them to a tunnel. In the tunnel, they are discovered by Earthmen who lead them further underground to the Black Knight, who tells Puddleglum, Eustace, and Jill of the queen of Underland's plan to take over a city above the ground where she will be queen and he will be king. The Black Knight also tells the search party that the queen binds him to a silver chair for one hour every night because he is under an enchantment that causes him to lose his mind during that time.

Unknown to the queen, the children decide to sit with the Black Knight during the hour of his enchantment. During that hour, he tells the children he is truly Prince Rilian under the evil spell of the queen. When he calls on the name of Aslan, which is the fourth sign, the children untie him, and the enchantment is broken. The queen returns to the room and throws mystical powder into the fireplace, which she uses to try to hypnotize them into forgetting Aslan and Narnia. Eustace and Jill almost forget, but Puddleglum stamps out the fire with his foot which breaks the spell and releases their minds from the wicked control of the queen. When the spell is broken, the queen turns into a snake, and Prince Rilian kills her.

The Earthmen, who the wicked queen had taken from the center of the earth to be slaves, return to their home in middle earth which is full of dazzling fire and glittering gems. Prince Rilian and his search crew follow tunnels to the surface of the earth where they discover they are directly under Narnia, the country the queen had planned to rule with Prince Rilian by her side.

Prince Rilian reunites with his father, the aged and ill King Caspian. (King Caspian is the king from the last two books of this series: *Prince Caspian* and *The Voyage of the DAWN TREADER).* Moments after the king and his son are reunited, the frail King Caspian dies. Aslan emerges, and he breathes on Eustace and Jill, which blows them out of Narnia to the mountain in Aslan's land.

King Caspian's body comes into view in the stream of Aslan's land. Aslan, who is in the form of a lion, has Eustace prick his paw with a thorn. Aslan lets his blood flow into the water and the king is resurrected to life. His old age and infirmity disappear, and he is once again a young, exuberant Caspian who throws his arms around Aslan in joy.

PART 2

DISCOVER THE ETERNAL PRINCIPLES

☞ **Teaching Point One: Meditate on God's Word.**

■ Read Psalm 119:92–104 and James 1:22–25. Read Chapter 2 where Aslan gives Jill the signs.

David said he would have perished in his affliction if it had not been for God's Word. Obedience to God's Word protects us from the consequences of sin. The Word gives us wisdom, understanding, and a desire for a strong mind and a resolute will to accomplish whatever God has for us to do. It also brings comfort and peace to our souls so that we are strengthened emotionally and spiritually by God's embracing truth, hope, and joy. David said he meditated on God's Word day and night, which made him wiser than his enemies and his teachers. God himself is our teacher when we study and meditate on the Bible. His Word is alive and active to comfort, convict, and reprove. God speaks to us intimately when we meditate on his Word.

By analogy, Aslan, the creator of Narnia, gave Jill four signs to follow. "These are the signs by which I will guide you in your quest," Aslan told Jill (Chapter 2). She was to memorize and meditate on them day and night. Jill failed to be diligent about this, however, and the negative consequences of her choice made the journey to rescue Prince Rilian longer, harder, and more dangerous.

Question 1: How were the signs that Aslan gave to Jill symbolic of God's Word? Give examples of how God's Word guides us today.

_____

_____

_____

_____

_____

_____

_____

_____

"Remember, remember, remember the signs. Say them to yourself when you wake in the morning and when you lie down at night, and when you wake in the middle of the night," Aslan told Jill (Chapter 2). Jill, however, did not always choose to follow Aslan's directions. The consequence of her choice was that the rescue party missed the first three signs which delayed their rescue and put them in danger of the giants.

Question 2: Why was it so important for Jill to be diligent to meditate on and remember the signs? Why did she stop reciting the signs to herself every day? How did the consequences of her actions negatively affect the rescue attempt, their safety, and her relationship with Aslan?

_____

_____

_____

_____

_____

Question 3: David said he meditated on God's law all day long. How should God's Word affect our thinking and decisions when we conscientiously focus on it throughout the day? What are the consequences of not knowing or of forgetting God's Word?

_____

_____

_____

✐ *Leader's Note: Ask the group for specific examples of creative and practical ways to meditate on God's Word throughout the day (example: music).*

Question 4: "Whatever strange things may happen to you, let nothing turn your mind from following the signs," Aslan told Jill (Chapter 2). Similarly, Hebrews 2:1 warns us to pay careful attention to what we have heard so that we do not drift away. What strange things happened along Jill, Eustace, and Puddleglum's journey that distracted them from following the signs? What can distract us or cause us to drift away from following God's laws today? How can we guard against drifting away according to the book of Hebrews?

_____

_____

_____

_____

_____

_____

Question 5: Aslan told Jill not to let the Narnian air confuse her mind. How can circumstances, hardships, or cultural beliefs confuse our minds if God's Word is not embedded in our heart, mind, and soul?

_____

_____

_____

Question 6: "Remember the signs and believe the signs. Nothing else matters," Aslan told Jill (Chapter 2). What did Aslan mean by this statement? Do you agree with Lewis's symbolism that the only thing that matters is remembering and believing God's Word? Defend your position.

_____

_____

_____

_____

Question 7: Jill, Eustace, and Puddleglum realized they had not succeeded in following Aslan's signs. When Rilian called on the name of Aslan, which was the fourth sign, the rescuers couldn't decide whether or not they should release him from the silver chair. "What had been the use of learning the signs if they weren't going to obey them?" they wondered (Chapter 11). The book of James tells us we need to look intently and continually at the law. Why are we tempted to listen to the Word, but not do what God tells us to do? The book of James says obedience to God's law brings freedom. How does obedience bring freedom? What does this imply about the consequences of disobedience?

_____

_____

_____

_____

_____

_____

_____

_____

_____

_____

☛ **Teaching Point Two: "To live is Christ, and to die is gain" (Philippians 1:21).**

■ Read Philippians 1:12-30 and Hebrews 2:15. Review chapters 13 and 14 in the text.

The apostle Paul was in prison. He did not know whether he would live or die, but he did know that his imprisonment was furthering the work of the Gospel and giving courage to other Christians to speak boldly for Christ. Paul's only aim was to courageously exalt Christ in his body in whatever way God chose to glorify himself, whether by Paul's life or by his death. If God still had work for Paul to do on earth, Paul vowed to live his life for Christ's glory. If God was ready to call Paul home, Paul knew the day of his death would be his day of final victory. Paul had been released from the slavery of the fear of death (Hebrews 2:15); therefore, he placed himself in the hands of God, willing to live or die for Christ.

"Doubtless," said Prince Rilian, "this signifies that Aslan will be our good lord, whether he means us to live or die." Prince Rilian echoed the words of the apostle Paul. C. S. Lewis reminded us through Rilian's words that even when we walk through the "valley of the shadow of death," God will be with us, so we do not need to fear (Psalm 23:4). God's loving kindness and goodness will surround us every day of our lives (Psalm 23:6).

Question 8: "And then, let us descend into the city and take the adventure that is sent us," Prince Rilian concluded after reminding Eustace, Jill, and Puddleglum that Aslan would be with them in life and in death (Chapter 13). How did Prince Rilian's belief that Aslan would be with them in life and death give him the courage to face the imminent danger of the Underland? How did Prince Rilian's words offer comfort to those with him?

_____

_____

_____

_____

Question 9: Why did the author of Hebrews 2:15 compare the fear of death to slavery? How does freedom from the fear of death change how we live our lives? Why is freedom from the fear of death essential to fully living our lives for Christ?

_____

_____

_____

_____

_____

_____

_____

Question 10: What will our lives look like if our daily purpose in life is to live for Christ? Give specific and practical examples.

_____

_____

_____

Question 11: What do believers gain when they die? Why did Paul say it was hard for him to choose if he would rather live or die?

_____

_____

_____

_____

☛ **Teaching Point Three: Trust God no matter what the circumstance or cost.**

■ Read Daniel 3:13–18. Review chapters 10, 11, and 12 in the text.

Nebuchadnezzar was enraged because Shadrach, Meshach, and Abednego refused to worship his golden image, so he gave them a frightening ultimatum: "Worship my gods, or be thrown into a furnace of blazing fire." Sarcasm and disbelief saturated his words as he asked, "Then what god will be able to rescue you from my hand?" (Daniel 3:15). The three men told Nebuchadnezzar that they knew their God was able to deliver them. Then Shadrach, Meshach, and Abednego declared their powerful proclamation of faith, "But even if He does not [rescue us], we want you to know, O king, that we will not serve your gods or worship the image of gold you have set up" (Daniel 3:18).

Eustace, Jill, and Puddleglum faced similar taunting. The Black Knight, who was Prince Rilian under an evil spell, mocked their faith in Aslan and ridiculed their belief in his guidance. The queen threw a powder into the fire to enchant Eustace, Jill, and Puddleglum into thinking that Aslan and Narnia were only figments of their childish imagination. Puddleglum stomped out the fire with his bare foot just before the witch's enchantment had gained complete control of them. This weakened the spell, and the pain from the burn cleared Puddleglum's thinking. He began to fight the spell with truth and faith. Puddleglum proclaimed to the queen, "I'm on Aslan's side even if there isn't any Aslan to lead it. I'm going to live as much like a Narnian as I can even if there isn't any Narnia" (Chapter 12). Puddleglum's proclamation of faith freed their minds from the evil control of the witch.

Question 12: How was Puddleglum's response similar to Shadrach, Meshach, and Abednego's statement of faith in God—regardless of their circumstances?

_____

_____

_____

_____

Question 13: How did Puddleglum put his faith into action to break the queen's spell? Why did Puddleglum need to act on his faith before the spell could be broken? What implications can you draw from this example?

_____

_____

_____

_____

Question 14: How was the queen's disbelief in Aslan similar to Nebuchadnezzar's disbelief in God? How were the queen's hypnotic suggestions, that Aslan and Narnia were all childish imagination, similar to the viewpoint of atheists today? Do you think Puddleglum's verbal response was a good one? Why or why not?

_____

_____

_____

_____

_____

_____

_____

Question 15: When Eustace explained to the Black Knight that Aslan had led them by the sign, "UNDER ME", which pointed them to the Underland, the knight laughed at them and gave a logical, historical explanation of why the land formed the words "UNDER ME". How does the secular world explain away God's creation, miracles, and guidance?

_____

_____

_____

_____

Question 16: "This was like cold water down the back to Scrubb and Jill; for it seemed to them very likely that the words had nothing to do with their quest at all, and that they had been taken in by a mere accident" (Chapter 10). How was Eustace and Jill's response different from Shadrach, Meshach, and Abednego's response? Why did the Black Knight's explanation shake Eustace and Jill's faith in Aslan? Would they have been better prepared for this attack on their faith if they had been diligent to meditate on the signs as Aslan had commanded?

_____

_____

_____

_____

_____

_____

_____

_____

Question 17: How can the secular world's scientific, historical, or logical explanations shake our faith? How should we respond if our faith is indeed shaken by the secular world's viewpoint?

_____

_____

_____

✐ *Leader's Note: Spend time in prayer and meditation on God's Word.*

Although the Black Knight's explanation shook the faith of Eustace and Jill, Puddleglum's faith remained firm. "There are no accidents," he proclaimed (Chapter 10). Puddleglum knew that even if the historical explanation for the words being carved were accurate, Aslan had been behind the formation—knowing years before the present time that Prince Rilian's rescue party would need them as a sign.

Question 18: How did Puddleglum's response demonstrate his faith in Aslan's sovereign working through history? Do you agree with the supposition that there are no accidents because God is in control of all circumstances?

_____

_____

_____

_____

_____

When Prince Rilian called on the name of Aslan, the children recognized it as the last sign for which Aslan had told them to look. "Do you mean you think everything will come right if we do untie him?" Eustace asked Puddleglum. "I don't know about that," was Puddleglum's reply. "You see, Aslan didn't tell Pole what would happen. He only told her what to do" (Chapter 11).

Question 19: Why did obedience to Aslan not guarantee that the three of them would be safe from harm? How did Puddleglum's response to Eustace compare to Shadrach, Meshach, and Abednego's response to King Nebuchadnezzar? Does God promise to keep our physical bodies safe from harm? What protection does God promise?

_____

_____

_____

_____

✎ *Leader's Note: He protects our souls (Psalm 49:15). He promises to work all things for our good and for His purpose (Romans 8:28).*

Question 20: Why should we, like Shadrach, Meshach, and Abednego, be willing to obey God no matter what the circumstance or the cost?

_____

_____

_____

_____

☛ **Teaching Point Four: We shall be raised imperishable.**

■ Read 1 Corinthians 15:35–55 and Isaiah 35:5–6. Review chapter 16 in the text.

When the last enemy, death, is destroyed and Christ returns, we will obtain our new bodies. Our heavenly body will not be like our earthly body. Our physical body is sown a perishable body, but it will be raised imperishable. It is sown in dishonor and weakness, but it will be raised in glory and power. Our natural body is buried, but our spiritual body will be raised from the dead. Our earthly bodies are like Adam—made from dust, and they cannot inherit heaven. Our heavenly bodies will be like Christ.

The lame will leap for joy, the blind will see, the deaf will hear. There will be no more pain or sorrow, and God will wipe every tear from our eyes. Our mortality will be swallowed up with immortality. Then we will declare, "Death has been swallowed up in victory!" (1 Corinthians 15:54).

C. S. Lewis gave us a picture of the resurrected body in the last chapter of *The Silver Chair*. King Caspian was resurrected from the dead in Aslan's land. Eustace and Jill had watched Caspian die in Narnia, but when they arrived in Aslan's land, Caspian's body appeared in the stream that had quenched Jill's thirst when she had first entered Narnia. Aslan asked Eustace to prick his paw with a thorn. Aslan's blood flowed into the stream, and Caspian rose from the dead. Caspian's new body was young, energetic, and strong. Caspian threw his arms around Aslan and greeted him with joy.

Question 21: What did the stream in Aslan's land symbolize? What was the symbolism of Aslan breathing on the children? Why did Aslan's blood resurrect Caspian's body? What did this symbolize?

_____

_____

_____

_____

_____

_____

_____

✐ *Leader's Note: The stream symbolizes the water of life (Revelation 22:17). Aslan's breath symbolized the breath of life (Genesis 2:7 and Acts 17:25). Aslan's blood symbolized Christ's blood, which covers our sins, allowing us entrance into the holy presence of God.*

Question 22: Caspian's resurrected body was youthful and strong. How does this compare to what Scripture says about our resurrected body?

_____

_____

_____

Question 23: What does Christ's resurrection tell us about our own promised resurrection? What do you think your resurrected body will be like? Support your answer with Scripture. How will our resurrected body be different from our earthly body?

_____

_____

_____

_____

_____

Question 24: How does Lewis's depiction of resurrection remind us that for believers "to die is gain" (Philippians 1:21)? Why should the knowledge of our future life with Christ empower us to live for Him each day?

_____

_____

_____

_____

PART 3

THE CLOSING CHAPTER

Eustace, Jill, and Puddleglum learned to trust and obey Aslan, no matter what the cost or circumstance. C. S. Lewis revealed Christ's victory over sin, evil, and death in this book about the victorious rescue of a prince from the evil queen of Underland. In the resurrection of King Caspian, we are reminded that we will one day proclaim with joy, "Where, O death, is your victory? Where, O death, is your sting?"(1 Corinthians 15:55).

Questions for the Closing Chapter

Question 1: How does the hope of resurrection and everlasting life with Christ comfort, challenge, or encourage you?

_____

_____

_____

Question 2: What does the Scripture "For me to live is Christ and to die is gain," mean to you (Philippians 1:21)

_____

_____

_____

Question 3: What did you find to be the most meaningful passage of this book? Why?

_____

_____

_____

Question 4: Which character(s) could you relate to the most? Why did you relate to him or her?

_____

_____

_____

Question 5: What new thoughts or insights do you have because you read this book? What additional themes or messages did you notice in this book?

_____

_____

_____

_____

Optional Activities

▲ *Ask the Lord to make you aware of new opportunities each day to live for Him, and then keep a journal of how He answers that prayer.*

▲ *Use your concordance and cross-referencing in your Bible to look up passages about Heaven.*

THE END OF THE BEGINNING

BOOK: THE LAST BATTLE

How does The Last Battle *symbolize Armageddon,
the return of Christ, and the new heaven and earth?*

C. S. Lewis completes *The Chronicles of Narnia* with *The Last Battle*, a tale that is an analogy of Armageddon, the return of Christ, and the new heaven and earth. This time the children from earth will not stop the evil that arises in Narnia. During Narnia's last battle, courage, valor, and faith end in martyrdom for those who are true followers of Aslan. C. S. Lewis takes us into eternity with the martyrs and gives us a glimpse of God's justice and the glories and joys of heaven. This final battle of Narnia reveals the everlasting victory of those who hope in Christ and endure to the end.

Unearthing the Deeper Meaning and Truth

How will the earth end? What will happen when Christ returns? What will heaven be like? This study will aid our understanding of the end times, the second coming of Christ, and the endless joy of eternity spent in the presence of God.

Scriptures:

Isaiah 65:17–25; Matthew 24:4–31; Matthew 25:1–10, 31–46; John 10:1–9; 2 Peter 3:10–18; 1 John 2:18–27; Revelation 6:12–17, 21:1–22:5.

Based on:

The Last Battle by C. S. Lewis (Scholastic Inc., 1956).

PART 1

BOOK SUMMARY: *THE LAST BATTLE*

✎ *Note to leader: Prior to the class, provide for each person the book, THE LAST BATTLE by C. S. Lewis.*

A selfish and cunning ape named Shift concocts a scheme to fool the Narnian creatures into believing Aslan has returned to Narnia and is reigning from a local stable. Shift dresses his donkey companion, Puzzle, in a lion skin to impersonate Aslan. Puzzle does not like the plan but has little confidence in his own decisions or intelligence. Shift joins forces with Rishda Tarkaan, a Calormene, and the evil spirit Tash. Together they rule with cruelty and force, all in the pseudonym of Aslan.

The Narnian creatures struggle to understand this change in Aslan, but they obey the orders given by the ape because they believe the orders come from Aslan, and they are confident Aslan knows best. However, the king of Narnia, Tirian, remembers Aslan's character and the stories of old. He recognizes there is something false about the reports of Aslan and his orders. Tirian calls on the true Aslan for help. The real Aslan summons Eustace and Jill, the children from *The Silver Chair*, back into Narnia to help with the pending battle.

The evil is so strong in Narnia that King Tirian recognizes this battle will probably be the last one for Narnia. Eustace, Jill, King Tirian, and the Narnians who are faithful to Aslan fight with courage and valor, knowing that they will likely die in the battle. The dwarfs of Narnia become cynical when they realize the "Aslan" in the stable is a fake, and they begin to fight against both sides, wallowing in doubt, disbelief, and selfishness as they shout, "The dwarfs are for the dwarfs."

The door of the stable that houses the false Aslan becomes a focal point of the battle when it becomes apparent that there is indeed a real God in the stable. Those that are evil and enter the stable door are consumed. Eventually, Eustace and Jill are forced through the door into the stable. They find themselves in brilliant light and peace, in the company of the former kings and queens of Narnia. Aslan greets them, and they realize they have crossed the line into eternity. They are now in a new Narnia.

In the New Narnia, the door of the stable stands completely alone and unsupported. It is the gateway between the old Narnia and everlasting life in the New Narnia. Aslan opens the door from eternity's side and calls into the black night of the old Narnia, "Now it is time!" Father Time awakens and blows his horn. The stars fall out of the sky. All the millions of Narnian creatures come running up to the doorway where Aslan stands, and they are forced to look Aslan in the face. Narnians who hate Aslan disappear to the left of the door. Those who are followers of Tash are swooped up in Tash's birdlike talons and disappear. The dwarves are locked in the darkness of their own disbelief, and they cannot see the New Narnia. The Narnians who love Aslan go through the door into the New Narnia. Aslan completely destroys the old Narnia.

The New Narnia is full of beauty, joy, and peace. All the characters that followed Aslan from former books of *The Chronicles of Narnia* are present. There is sweet and blessed reunion with all. Thus end the tales of Narnia and begin the adventures of eternity.

Part 2

Discover the Eternal Principles

☞ **Teaching Point One: In the last hour, we must beware of false teachers.**

■ Read Matthew 24:4–27 and 1 John 2:18–27.

The Book of Matthew warns us that many will claim to be the Christ, and they will try to mislead us. False prophets will arise who are liars and deceivers who mix half-truths with lies in an attempt to deceive, if it were possible, even the elect (Matthew 24:24). The Book of Matthew tells us that when Christ returns, it will be like lightening that flashes across the sky (v.27)! There will be no uncertainty about whom Christ is when He comes.

The Book of 1 John tells us we are in the last hour. God's timing is not like our timing. A thousand years are like a day to the Lord (2 Peter 3:8). Though this last hour seems like a long time to us, God is not slow about keeping His promise to return. He is patient, not wishing any to perish, but everyone to come to repentance (2 Peter 3:9). We do not know the day or the hour that Christ will return, but we must always be vigilantly ready.

Question 1: How did the ape, Rishda Tarkaan, and the ginger cat depict the false prophets or antichrist(s) described in the book of Matthew? How did they mix truth with lies to deceive the Narnians? Lewis said, "By mixing a little truth with it they had made their lie stronger" (Chapter 9). How do false teachers today mix truth with lies? Give examples.

_____

_____

_____

_____

_____

_____

_____

_____

Question 2: Matthew 24:9 speaks of a time of persecution. How did C. S. Lewis portray this in his tale about Narnia?

_____

_____

_____

_____

Question 3: Matthew 24:10 tells us many will turn away from the faith. They will betray and hate each other. How did the dwarfs represent this group of people? Why did the dwarfs turn away from the faith? Why did they hate allies of Aslan as well as the false god Tash? What were the results of their disbelief?

_____

_____

_____

_____

_____

_____

Question 4: Matthew 24:13 tells us that those who stand firm to the end will be saved. In _The Last Battle,_ who represented those who stood firm to the end? How were they saved? What was the reward for their courage and endurance?

_____

_____

_____

_____

Question 5: At first, Tirian was confused by the reports of "Aslan." When he remembered Aslan's character and how Aslan had worked in Narnia throughout history, however, Tirian knew the evil reports about Aslan were false. Why did this help King Tirian recognize the reports about Aslan were false?

_____

_____

_____

_____

Question 6: God is the same yesterday, today, and forever (Hebrews 13:8). With this verse in mind, why should remembering what God has done throughout history strengthen our faith? How do Bible stories aid in this process? How can remembering who God is, and all that He has done, keep us from doubting and disbelief?

Question 7: How may dwelling on Christ's character keep us from being deceived by false teachers who mix lies with truth? How does Scripture knowledge guard and protect us from false teaching?

Question 8: Tirian called on the true Aslan for help. No immediate help came, but "… there began to be a kind of change inside Tirian. Without knowing why, he began to feel a faint hope. And he felt somehow stronger" (Chapter 4). Why did Tirian begin to have hope? How does prayer change us, even if God does not change our circumstances?

☛ **Teaching Point Two: Jesus is the door to eternal life.**

■ Read Matthew 25:1–10, 31–46 and John 10:1–9. Review Chapters 12 and 13 in the text.

Matthew 25 warns us to be ready for Christ's return. Jesus told us in the parable of the ten virgins, that those who were ready for the bridegroom went in with him to the wedding banquet, and the door was closed. Those that were not ready when he arrived could say or do nothing to open the door. They were too late. Matthew 24:32–35 tells us that when we see the signs of the second coming, we will know Christ is near, right at the door. Jesus said, "I am the door; if anyone enters through Me, he shall be saved.…" (John 10:9 NASV).

C. S. Lewis used an actual door into the New Narnia to symbolize the truths of these passages. All the Narnian creatures came up to Aslan as he stood in the doorway. They had no choice but to look straight into Aslan's face. When some looked at Aslan, their faces became full of fear and hate. These creatures swerved to Aslan's left and disappeared into his shadow to the left of the doorway. They found themselves in darkness and misery or swept away by the talons of the false god Tash. They were never seen again. Others looked into Aslan's face and loved him, though some were frightened. All of these entered through the door on Aslan's right into the bright light, peace, and joy of the New Narnia.

Lewis used this symbolism to remind us to be ready for Christ's return. "Therefore keep watch, because you do not know the day or the hour" (Matthew 25:13). Matthew 25:31–33 tells us that when Jesus comes in His glory, the nations will be gathered before Him. He will separate them as a shepherd separates sheep from goats. To those on the right Jesus will say, "Come, you who are blessed by My Father; take your inheritance, the kingdom prepared for you since the creation of the world" (Matthew 25:34). To those on the left he will say, "Depart from Me, you who are cursed, into the eternal fire prepared for the devil and his angels" (Matthew 25:41).

Question 9: "Tirian looked and saw the queerest and most ridiculous thing you can imagine. Only a few yards away, clear to be seen in the sunlight, there stood up a rough wooden door and, round it, the framework of the doorway: nothing else, no walls, no roof. The door was simply standing up by itself as if it had grown there like a tree" (Chapter 13). What do you think the stable door represented? Explain your answer.

_____

_____

_____

_____

_____

_____

Question 10: "'Yes,' said Queen Lucy. 'In our world too, a stable once had something inside it that was bigger than our whole world'" (Chapter 13). What was the symbolism of the door being a stable door?

_____

_____

_____

_____

✎ *Leader's Note: Jesus was born in a stable. It represented the place where salvation was found through Christ.*

Question 11: Aslan went to the door and roared, "'Now it is time!' then louder, 'time!'; then so loud that it could have shaken the stars 'TIME.' The door flew open" (Chapter 13). To what time did this passage refer? What did the coming of Father Time represent?

_____

_____

_____

_____

✎ *Leader's Note: The second coming of Christ. Father Time represented the end of the world as we know it and Christ's return.*

Question 12: How does C. S. Lewis's analogy compare and contrast to the passage in Matthew 25? Who do the Narnian creatures that entered the door represent? Who do the creatures that went to the left of Aslan and the door represent?

_____

_____

Question 13: "Shut the door." Aslan told high King Peter. Peter took out a golden key and locked the door. How does this compare to the analogy Jesus told of the bridegroom shutting the door? What was the symbolism of the door being locked?

_____

_____

_____

_____

✐ *Leader's Note: The opportunity for salvation was over.*

Question 14: "All of the old Narnia that mattered, all the dear creatures, have been drawn into the real Narnia through the door" (Chapter 15). What things on earth matter and will last for eternity? What things on earth do not matter in the face of eternity?

_____

_____

_____

_____

Question 15: How is Jesus our door to eternity? (Consider John 14:6) How do we enter the door that is Jesus? What did Jesus mean when He said that He is The Door?

_____

_____

_____

_____

_____

_____

✐ *Leader's Note: He is the only way to salvation.*

Question 16: After the final battle, Aslan met Tirian in the New Narnia. "Well done, last of the Kings of Narnia who stood firm at the darkest hour" (Chapter 13). How should we live our lives so that we can hear, "Well done, good and faithful servant" (Matthew 25:21)?

_____

_____

_____

☛ **Teaching Point Three: Christ is coming to earth again.**

■ Read Matthew 24:29–31, 2 Peter 3:10–18, and Revelation 6:12–17. Review chapter 14 in the text.

After the "distress of those days," there will be a great earthquake. The sun will be darkened, the moon will become like blood and give no light, and the stars will fall from the sky like fruit falls from a tree in a great wind. The sky will split apart and every mountain and island will be moved out of its place. Then the Son of Man will appear in the sky riding on the clouds. Christ's angels will go forth with a trumpet sound, and they will gather the elect from the four winds, from one end of the heavens to the other.

When Aslan appeared in Narnia, the stars fell out of the sky, and the sun was twenty times its normal size and dark red. The moon was also red and in the wrong position. Narnia was at an end.

Question 17: How does Lewis's description of the coming of Aslan and the end of Narnia compare and contrast to Christ's return and the end of the Earth as we know it?

_____

_____

_____

_____

_____

Question 18: When Christ returns, why do you think men will cry out for the rocks to fall on them to hide them from Christ's presence (Revelation 6:16)? How will the end of the earth be evidence of the wrath of the Lamb? Why should this passage be a warning to all mankind?

_____

_____

_____

_____

_____

■ *Answer the following questions based on 2 Peter 3:10–18:*

Question 19: What does this passage mean when it says the day of the Lord will come like a thief (v.10)?

_____

_____

Question 20: How will the earth be destroyed?

_____

_____

Question 21: According to the book of 2 Peter, how can we hasten the coming of Christ (v.11–12)?

_____

_____

Question 22: Why should knowing these passages beforehand help us to be on guard against evil? How can being carried away by the error of lawless men make us fall from our secure position?

_____

_____

Question 23: Which characters in *The Final Battle* remained steadfast? What was their reward? Which characters did not remain steadfast? What were their consequences?

_____

_____

_____

_____

_____

☛ **Teaching Point Four: There will be a new heaven and a new earth.**

■ Read Isaiah 65:17–25 and Revelation 21:1–22:5. Review passages in the text from the end of chapters 12 to the end of the book that refer to the New Narnia.

According to God's promise, we are looking for a new heaven and a new earth in which righteousness is triumphant. The brilliant beauty and overwhelming joy of the New Jerusalem is more than we can think or imagine (Ephesians 3:20). Its foundation will be precious jewels of dazzling hues. The city will be pure gold like clear glass, and its gates of pearl will never close. There will be no more death, mourning, or weeping because there will be no more sin or evil. Peace will dwell in all of God's new creation. God himself will be our light, and there will be no night. God's name will be on our foreheads, and he will dwell among us. We will glorify Him forever with gladness and rejoicing.

In *The Last Battle*, C. S. Lewis's characters realized their beloved Narnia was only a shadow of the real Narnia that had no beginning or end, just as our earth is a shadow of the new heaven and earth that God promises to his children. Lewis's noble unicorn spoke the words that were on the hearts of all the Narnians who had entered this glorious new Narnia. "I have come home at last! This is my real country! I belong here. This is the land I have been looking for all my life." (Chapter 15)

Lewis's tender and joyous portrayal of the reunion of all of the Narnians who had gone before Jill and Eustace reminds us of our own yearning desire to see those we love who have gone before us into eternity. Lewis also gives us a glimpse of the pure excitement and joy we will have when we meet the patriarchs of our faith. Lewis attempted to give us a foretaste of the joys of eternity that God has in store for those whose names are written in the Lamb's Book of Life because of their repentance and belief in Christ as their precious Lord and Savior.

Question 24: The Bible tells us we are aliens on this earth (Hebrews 11:13). How did the unicorn's statement about the new Narnia symbolize the joyous sense of finally being home that we will have once we reach heaven's shores? What does Scripture mean when it says we are aliens on this earth? What perspective should this give us?

_____

_____

_____

_____

Question 25: Heaven will have no sin, sorrow, mourning, crying, or death. How will our lives be drastically different because of the absence of sin and death? Give practical examples. (Consider our own sin nature, how sin affects relationships with other people and nations, and the effects sin has on creation.)

_____

_____

_____

_____

_____

Question 26: Why do you think the gates of heaven will never be closed?

_____

_____

Question 27: Why will there no longer be any night? What will be the source of our light? What does this imply about God?

_____

_____

_____

_____

Question 28: What will be the cause of our rejoicing and gladness?

_____

_____

Question 29: What promises about heaven are most precious to you? Why?

_____

_____

_____

_____

_____

_____

PART 3

THE CLOSING CHAPTER

The Last Battle is an analogy of Armageddon, the end of the earth, and the new Heaven and a new earth. Through its tale of both justice and eternal joy, there is an underlying warning to all of Lewis's readers. Be ready! We do not know the day nor the hour of the Lord's return. Enter through the door of salvation that is Jesus. Be faithful and courageous to the end to see our eternal reward and forever be in the presence of our dear Lord and Savior, Jesus.

Questions for the Closing Chapter

Question 1: Have you gone through the door that is Jesus? Have you come to Him in repentance and belief, desiring to follow and obey Him? Explain your answer.

_____

_____

_____

_____

Question 2: Are you anxious for Jesus to return to earth? How can we be ready for His return?

_____

_____

_____

Optional Activities

▲ *If you have never decided to follow Christ as your Lord and Savior, pray now asking for His forgiveness and telling Him you want to live your life in obedience to Him.*

▲ *Make a point to share the love, joy, and hope of Christ with those you come in contact with every day so that they, too, will be ready to receive God's offer of salvation and eternal life through Jesus Christ.*

Additional Resources

ChristianBibleStudies.com

Heaven, Randy Alcorn (Tyndale House, 2004; ISBN: 0842379428)

Heaven: My Father's House, Anne Graham Lotz (Thomas Nelson/W, 2005; ISBN: 0849917484)

One Minute After You Die: A Preview of Your Final Destination, Erwin Lutzer (Moody Publishers, 1997; ISBN: 0802463223)

Second Coming of Christ, Charles Spurgeon (Whitaker House, 1996; ISBN: 0883683806)

The Power of Christ's Second Coming, Charles Spurgeon (Ywam Publishing, 1996; ISBN: 1883002206)

The Second Coming: Signs of Christ's Return and the End of the Age, John MacArthur (Good News Publishing, 2006; ISBN: 158134757X)